ZERO
REGRETS

Meli Casey

Foreword by Patti Johnson,
CEO of PeopleResults,
Author of *"Make Waves: Be the One to Start Change at Work and in Life"*

COPYRIGHT

Copyright © 2019 Meli Casey. All rights reserved.

Cover Design by Joreld Dhamo

Internal Book Designs by Joreld Dhamo

Author Photograph by James Edward

Foreword by Patti Johnson

Edited by Copy Write Consultants, LLC

ISBN: 9781091833562
Published by Amazon Kindle Direct Publishing (June 2019)

To my baby . . .

May you live a wonderful and happy life

where you are clear about your choices

and free to live a life with Zero Regrets.

To anyone who was ever told that things can't change or

that you can't do something . . .

no matter what your circumstances are,

remember that you always have choices.

May you find them and change your

future for the better.

ACKNOWLEDGEMENTS

To my husband, who is my rock and true partner in life, day in and day out through all the ups and downs in life—thank you from the bottom of my heart for always being there. In addition, my son and my stepdaughters were instrumental in supporting me through this process. Special thanks to Maddie who made me realize this was possible with a little bit of dedication and discipline.

In addition, thanks to my little brother, Ry, who has always believed in me and never questioned my advice and counsel—no matter how crazy it may have seemed at the time. Thanks for making me feel like you're my biggest fan and reminding me even in the hard times that we can always find some "awesomeness" inside.

Thanks to my parents, family, friends, and coworkers who continue to inspire me, energize me, and motivate me to follow my dreams and always think big. I believe because you believe. And lastly, a heartfelt thanks to Patti for helping me find my "wave" and push through my own mental barriers.

<u>FOREWORD</u>

By Patti Johnson
CEO of PeopleResults,
Author of *"Make Waves: Be the One to Start Change at Work and in Life"*

It's too easy to get caught up in what we are "supposed to do" in life and the world's definition of success rather than our own. I fell into that trap early in my career. I wish I had this book years ago to help me define my priorities and purpose. Zero Regrets is that kind of book.

Meli brings her own unique perspective and experiences on how to live a purposeful life. She guides you through this personal exploration chapter by chapter and page by page. You can almost hear her voice as if you are having an informal conversation with a mentor or coach. And, I often saw myself in her relatable stories and examples.

Zero Regrets starts from the inside out – rather than the other way around. First, you explore your values and become more self-aware of your gifts and talents. You then move into the impact of relationships and how we spend our time. There are also important exercises to identify what we can control and influence – and, also, accepting what we cannot.

The purpose of the book is to encourage you to stop, think and be intentional. There are exercises to help you define your unique purpose and dreams that go well beyond salary, job title or earning the top performance rating. We are whole entire beings with careers, families, friends and communities where we live. Therefore, a 'Zero Regrets' definition of success must include our entire life not just one side of us.

Meli also encourages us not to think of our goals as "yes" or "no" propositions. There are typically many options between "yes, start now" and "no, you can't". Consider all the possibilities in between – such as, "maybe", "partially", or "later". A path for incremental progress or a new creative option may open a new door that you thought was closed.

How we spend our time and who we spend our time with has an enormous impact on reaching our goals. Zero Regrets shares that while being intentional with our time – we can also be creative. Busy lives can be enhanced by blending priorities, such as social time with friends and family or combining a work team event with a community service event. Creativity and intention can produce new ideas you may not have considered.

This book provides a wonderful blend of finding your purpose through practical strategies and exercises to help you stop, think and reframe. As an example, I read the section on "What Myths Have You Been Living?" twice as I considered the conflicts between our values and what is often expected from us at an early age. We value speaking up and being honest, yet we learn as children to be respectful and not make waves. Identifying these internal conflicts can play an essential role in our personal growth.

The exercises push your thinking through straightforward and direct questions. This combination approach encouraged me to slow down and rediscover my goals, a fresh perspective and remember the blind spots that could get in my way.

I'm a big believer in taking the first step toward the changes you want in your life or "making waves". Zero Regrets sets the foundation for actually starting a change through self-reflection.

This is a book to savor, spend time with, write in, underline and help you stop and really think. Take one chapter at a time and write down your answers and even go back to them. Slow down and do this for yourself.

Get started now on living your version of life with Zero Regrets!

INTRODUCTION

What does it mean to live a life with Zero Regrets? It doesn't mean that your life should be perfect or that you would never make any mistakes. The idea of having a life with Zero Regrets means that you can live your life knowing with a clear conscience that **you've made the best choices with the information you knew and the options you had in the moment**—and you can focus on enjoying your life now. It's also the idea that you **didn't leave any opportunities behind**— you explored, you learned, you loved, and above all, you lived.

We all have choices. While circumstances occur that we have no control over—what happens *afterward* is usually a matter of choices and decisions that we *do* have complete control over. In this book, I share stories about family, personal growth, and professional development. My goal is go guide you through reflection and thought-provoking questions to push your thinking and encourage you to take the Zero Regrets Challenge.

I won't pretend to be perfect, and I'll admit that I have not always been clear around what my choices were either. We all have times when our mind only shows us "limited" options, especially when there is high stress or low confidence; but with practice, discipline and conviction, we can all build a growth mindset that expands those options and choices.

My journey to Zero Regrets started on the evening of December 26, 2005, after a conversation with my grandma, "Tita," during my holiday vacation in Mexico. But first, let me tell you a little bit about my Tita.

My Tita was raised in Saltillo, Mexico by a family with very low income in a time when our culture was very traditional. She was only able to make it to the second grade in school, which was one more year in education than my grandpa got . . . and then she married my grandpa, with whom she was madly in love, at the age of eighteen.

This particular Christmas we had spent time with my siblings, cousins, and family in Mexico, as we had for many years. The day after, my grandpa suffered a stroke that led him to be taken immediately to the hospital.

During the hours that followed, our family thought the time had come to say goodbye and prepare ourselves for the worst-case scenario.

My task that night was to take my Tita back to her house and take care of her. She was in frail condition and would not be able to handle endless hours in the hospital as we awaited what fate would bring. I still remember her tears would not stop rolling down her face, and the best support I could provide was to hold her hand and give her hugs as she told me many stories.

In what seemed like an endless night, I spent a long time listening and talking to Tita as she felt like her world would end that night if my grandpa passed away. At this point, she had been married to him for sixty-four years—a total lifetime.

That single conversation had a lasting impact in my life. My Tita expressed regret after regret after regret that she had in her life. How was it that in such a vulnerable, sad, and scary moment, all she could think about was all the regrets she had in her life instead of all the happy moments they had and all the things she should've been thankful for?

I started picturing myself being eighty-two years old, and I was *terrified* at the idea that I might live my life in a way that would only end in a multitude of regrets. After that night there were many days and nights of reflection over many years before I would develop my vision and plan for how I would make sure I lived a life with **ZERO REGRETS.**

The journey hasn't been perfect, and years after this night I ended up hitting my own "rock bottom," a moment I remember very vividly. It felt like I had lost myself completely due to a series of bad choices. The last few strings that I had holding me together were gone, and I had no idea where I would begin rebuilding.

Luckily, I found myself surrounded by support from unexpected places. One step at a time, I started putting my puzzle pieces together. What kept me grounded was my determination to start over and lead a life that made me happy every day.

I don't have any magic dust in this book that will be life-altering. However, the lessons you will read about might bring you some new insights into how resilience, determination, and focus can help you achieve your goals. And the questions I ask you to reflect on could bring you a new awareness to enhance your potential or minimize your challenges.

The lessons and activities in this book center around the principle that you must first have a strong foundation with a healthy mind, body, and soul. Once these are balanced and in good shape, then you elevate to focus on your legacy and ultimately to make your dreams come true.

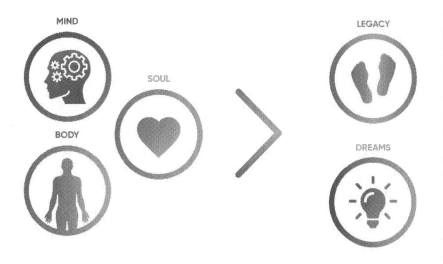

What I hope is that there are a few takeaways that you can get out of reading about these **CHOICES** that you *do* have control over so that you also can live a life with Zero Regrets and improve your quality of life both personally and professionally.

When you finish reading these choices, take the Zero Regrets Challenge and start your personal transformation. As you make progress, find ways to pay it forward and help others around you to enhance their life as well. Together, we can lift each other. Are you ready?

CHOICE 1 - VALUES

 How you define yourself influences the

glasses the world sees you through...

Values are a funny thing. When I talk to others about values, some interpret values as something you inherit from your family, from your upbringing or from your surroundings, while others believe that they are never permanent and that you can always model and change them. And of course, there are values based on religious beliefs too. I respect any and all views that you might have, because I acknowledge we all have different starting points based on our unique life experiences.

As we start this journey, it's important to note that there is no right or wrong answer to the questions I will ask you. You will need to search within yourself to choose which answers best meet your needs so that you can lead a life with Zero Regrets.

Story Part 1: Losing Axton in the Woods

When Axton turned twenty-eight, he and his best friend Niosh went camping in the woods. They celebrated the end of a long workweek and were relieved to escape the hustle and bustle of New York life . . . as well as the bore of the daily routine.

Axton and Niosh had been friends for four years and shared everything together. They had supported each other through relationship ups and downs, job loss, and family challenges.

They were both very different people who happened to enjoy the outdoors. Niosh constantly worked out but ate mostly fast food—something his parents got him used to from a young age. He was proud of his heritage and education and was always looking to get ahead.

Axton, on the other hand, was constantly on the run but always making time for healthy food. He was a social butterfly and a free spirit—letting the wind dictate where he would go next.

(continued)

After a couple hours of hiking, they found the ideal spot to spend the night. In casual conversation, Niosh shared with Axton that he was thinking about going back to school to get his MBA. Axton shyly smiled and tried to change the subject. Niosh, however, insisted on staying on topic and even suggested that Axton join him, so they could pursue their MBAs together.

What Niosh didn't know was that Axton had never finished his bachelor's degree. In the time they'd known each other, they had discussed which schools each of them had attended, but Axton had never felt comfortable telling Niosh that he didn't finish his degree.

When Axton was in his third year of college, his mother had become very ill. Since he was an only child. and his parents had divorced when he was young, he had felt the need to drop out of college to take care of her.

(continued)

He had always regretted that decision, because he never got around to going back to school after his mother's health improved. He had been extremely embarrassed and had preferred to keep it as private as possible.

Soon after returning home after the camping trip, Axton stopped hanging out with Niosh, and their relationship started to fade until they no longer spoke to each other. Axton regretted that too.

WHO ARE YOU?

Like Axton and Niosh, we all have a story that leads us to who we are today. Through ups and downs, we've made decisions along the way that started painting the picture of our life.

If someone were to ask you, "Who are you, really?" how would you respond? There are many layers that might describe who each of us is, and I'll describe a few examples for you to start considering . . .

Who you are *physically*—This layer tends to be the most obvious to others around you. Your choices in clothing, your hair style, your makeup, whether you work out or not are all examples of the first thing someone *might* notice about you. These may or may not be grounded in your values or beliefs.

For Niosh, these were all sacred: he spent a lot of time exploring which choices he would make on a daily basis to ensure they represented something. Axton spent the time based on what he thought others wanted or expected to see. And there are also others who believe that these things are superficial and don't mean anything. No matter where you are on the spectrum, and no matter what you think—you are making choices daily that fit somewhere in the spectrum.

Who you are *socially*—This layer, depending on circumstances, may also be rather obvious to some around you. Everyone around Axton knew he was in a relationship, who his close friends were, how friendly he was, what organizations he was involved in—these are the types of things one *might* hear about you. These, again, may have happened by pure chance, or you might have specific values that you lean on that drive your responses to some of these questions.

For example, Niosh had many relationships that stemmed from shared religious beliefs; he also stopped socializing with some people due to a lack of shared values. For many of us, these started organically in life and through experience, we started filtering our options and choices.

Who you are *on paper*—Your credentials may also be documented, published, or otherwise readily available. Niosh's job, job title, some accomplishments, and education were all available publicly. There may be similar things available for you that you either want or would prefer not to be documented. While you had choices and decisions that led to all of these, the most important thing to remember is that you still have choices and options about what starts happening today.

WHAT DEFINES YOU?

Axton let his unfinished education define him. He held the value of education in such high regard that he was embarrassed about not meeting his own expectations. He was so embarrassed, in fact, that he let it impact his relationship with Niosh.

Niosh, on the other hand, was very confused and disappointed about Axton fading away without any explanation. He assumed Axton just didn't support him in getting a higher education and developing himself. What Axton didn't know was that Niosh was the first in his family to get a bachelor's degree. If Axton had shared his situation, Niosh would've been very understanding and supportive, helping him grow his career in other ways.

Axton is not alone. Many of us have insecurities in one or several areas of our lives. However, that doesn't mean that we should let them define who we are and how we live for the rest of our lives. I am a firm believer that however you answered the question about who you are, *YOU can still control HOW and WHEN you let it define you, if at all*.

This is one of the biggest choices you must make in life. While you can't change your past experiences or what you have and haven't done, you can start a new life *any day you choose*. That means that no matter what your upbringing looked like, what your surroundings have been like—you can always change.

That's not to say that it will be easy. Unless you are very clear what your values are, your choices may not be clear. Here is an activity I would encourage you to complete as part of your journey to Zero Regrets.

Activity: Defining Your Values

Part 1 - *Make your own list of the values that are most important to you. Here are some of the most common ones to get you started:*

1. Integrity (Ethics, Honesty, Respect)
2. Excellence (Quality, Performance, Aesthetics)
3. Collaboration (Cooperation, Support)
4. Achievement (Results, Success)
5. Fairness (Inclusion, Compassion)
6. Tradition (Sensitivity, Humility, Service)
7. Innovation (Creativity, Curiosity, Improvement)

_____   _____   _____
_____   _____   _____
_____   _____   _____
_____   _____   _____
_____   _____   _____
_____   _____   _____
_____   _____   _____

Part 2 — *Circle the ones you would uphold no matter what and reflect on any exceptions.*

Activity: Defining Your Legacy

Part 1 — *Imagine that you passed away and a documentary is created in your memory. To start writing the plot of the movie, what THREE WORDS would you use to describe the legacy you left behind. Next, what two or three accomplishments would you want to be highlighted as your major life achievements?*

Legacy Left Behind:
1. _____
2. _____
3. _____

Accomplishments:
1. _____
2. _____
3. _____

Part 2 — *It's said that people don't remember what you say, but they remember how you made them feel. In developing this documentary, many people are interviewed: 1) some that played a key role in your life, 2) some that you crossed paths with briefly, and 3) some that were indirectly impacted by your decisions. Write down the words or sentences you would want each of these groups to use when describing you and the legacy you left behind.*

_____	_____	_____
_____	_____	_____
_____	_____	_____
_____	_____	_____
_____	_____	_____

WHAT MYTHS HAVE YOU BEEN LIVING?

Remember that this is a journey of discovery before we can move to concrete changes. The subconscious mind works in mysterious ways and sometimes we need clues and passwords to unlock its secret information.

It took me many years before I realized that I was having internal conflict because some of my beliefs or values were in sharp conflict with one another. Here is a list of examples that I've collected from my own experiences as well as from others around me. It shows how things we've been told or taught (whether right or not) might be in conflict with your overarching values.

- <u>Strong value in being honest; yet:</u>
  - o Taught that you should always agree with senior leaders or those in charge, even if you disagree.

- Taught to not make a big deal at a restaurant if something doesn't meet your expectations—so withhold sharing any complaints or concerns.
- Taught to not hurt people's feelings, so it's best to not be entirely honest.

- <u>Strong value in being respectful; yet:</u>
  - Taught that speaking while elders are in the room was not respectful; but yet, if you don't speak up, you're seen as not having an opinion at work.
  - Taught to not interrupt others; but yet, if you only have official conversations with others at work, you're seen as not being social or collaborative enough.

- <u>Strong value in connecting with others; yet:</u>
  - Taught to not discuss religion, politics, intimate matters, or financial position with anyone.
  - Taught to not share any weakness, private conflicts, challenges, or limitations with others because they will think negatively of you.
  - Taught to not become friends or socialize with others from work because it is not appropriate.

- <u>Strong value in being yourself; yet:</u>
    - Taught to not wear anything at work that might make you stand out because it's distracting.
    - Taught to only speak in certain ways that make you sound like those in senior positions.
    - Taught that you must always dress up when you go out—even to the grocery store.

Story Part 2: Losing Axton in the Woods

Thirteen years later, Axton got engaged, and the first person he could think of to be his best man was Niosh. He had always regretted how their friendship had ended, so he called him out of the blue to meet at a coffee shop.

As he was waiting for his coffee, he heard a familiar voice say, "Axton?" He turned around and was excited to see Niosh standing behind him.

(continued)

Axton and Niosh sat and drank their coffee together. They exchanged stories and laughed like in their earlier days. Then Niosh's expressions changed a bit and looked sad. Niosh asked Axton, "Axton, what happened to our friendship? I never understood why you stopped talking to me."

Axton sighed and explained "I know . . . I was young and confused. Do you remember the time we went camping? You were trying to convince me to get an MBA with you." "Yes, I remember. You seemed to get upset after that," said Niosh.

"Well, what you didn't know was that I had not completed my bachelor's degree yet. I was embarrassed to admit it and didn't really want anyone to know."

"However, a couple years later, I got my act together and went back to school. It took me a few years to finish my degree on the side, but I did it! I was inspired by you, and I got tired of letting my lack of education define who I was. However, it was important enough that I made it a priority to complete it once and for all."

(continued)

"Oh, wow!" exclaimed Niosh. "I had no idea. I'm so sorry. I must've put you in a very awkward position. I never meant to hurt your feelings. You were my best friend."

Axton and Niosh reconciled and Niosh agreed to be Axton's best man. Finally—one decision at a time and Axton felt like his major regrets were now long gone.

Chapter Summary

As a recap of everything we just covered, remember that while there are many layers that might explain who you are today, you get to choose what will define you in the future.

Take the time to acknowledge your values, pressure-test them, and ensure you have clarity about which ones you will prioritize over others. Also, question the unspoken rules that might be in conflict and make some choices today that will make you feel great tomorrow.

The constant push and pull between your own beliefs and those that you might have been taught by parents, teachers, religious figures, friends, and other social influences can be downright exhausting. The sooner you realize what unspoken rules you've been following that might be in conflict with your other beliefs, the sooner you can start making intentional choices about how you will handle each situation once and for all.

CHOICE 2 - SELF-AWARENESS

 When you turn the microscope inward, you uncover a world of possibilities . . .

The second choice you have is being aware about who you are and how you are perceived. Just because you know who you are—your name, what you look like, what you like or don't like—doesn't mean that you know truly what your strengths and limits are, why you think the way you do, why you do what you do, or why or how others perceive you the way they do. These are all choices to uncover.

You need to get grounded in your values before you can explore your choices in self-awareness. This typically starts with some level of personal vulnerability. Brené Brown describes it best in her book *Daring Greatly* (Brown, 2012) when she says, "Vulnerability sounds like truth and feels like courage. Truth and courage aren't always comfortable, but they're never weakness." You must be willing to brave the water and become exposed.

Story Part 1: Controlled by a Blind Spot

Tyra and her two brothers grew up moving around from one home to another across the country. Her father was in the military, and her mother devoted her life to raising her children. Both of her parents were strict and had high expectations for their children.

When Tyra got older, she got a great job as a nurse in a small hospital in her town. She married a lawyer and had three kids to raise at home. However, even though she was successful at work, she felt overworked. At home, she felt like no matter how much she did, the house was always a mess and felt like they were living paycheck to paycheck. It was never enough.

One day, Tyra was working with one of her new patients in the hospital. The patient had experienced a significant injury to his leg and needed to consider his options.

(continued)

Tyra proceeded to share with her patient and his sister all the details about the different procedures, hoping to influence them to have surgery.

Out of nowhere, the patient's sister yelled at Tyra, "Stop! What is wrong with you? He's not a robot. Don't you know how painful this is for him?" Tyra didn't know what to say. She was simply telling them their options and wanted to make sure they had all the information they needed to make their decision.

Later that day, she got approached by one of the lead doctors. He asked her to take a walk with him and proceeded to tell her: "Tyra, I heard about what happened with your patient today. You're bright, but everyone thinks of you as being cold and impersonal with your patients. We can't keep having patients complain about you like this."

(continued)

Tyra was an introvert and shy in general. She listened to what the doctor said, but words to respond couldn't come to mind, so she just listened and stayed quiet.

"Why do they think that?" she thought to herself. Then she pictured moments with her family and friends. She cared so much about people, and that was the reason she had wanted to become a nurse. It didn't make sense that everyone had this perception of her. What was she missing?

Tyra is not alone. Many of us have blind spots in our self-awareness that may or may not be evident yet. Let's start by searching within before we search outside of ourselves. For this section, I'll focus on the three components of Self-Awareness that have made the biggest impact in my life: 1) What are my strengths? 2) How am I perceived? 3) Why do I do what I do? and 4) How can I narrow down my gaps?

WHAT ARE YOUR STRENGTHS?

Once you have identified your values and grounded yourself on what you want to define you, you need to be clear on what your strengths are. I've known many people that go through life simply "by chance"—letting the wind determine which way they blow.

If you want to live an intentional life, you must choose to be clear about your strengths so that you can maximize your use of those. Tyra was definitely clear about one of her strengths. She knew she had good attention to detail, which helped her notice signs in patients, quantities, and subtleties that might not be obvious to others.

For you, let's start with a basic activity to get some ideas of what your strengths are.

Activity: Defining Your Strengths

"My Awesome Self" Create a short email survey and send it to friends, family, and coworkers or clients you work with.

Ask them for these things:

1) What are words that describe what you admire in me?

_____   _____   _____

_____   _____   _____

_____   _____   _____

2) Share one or two stories of when I was awesome and why?

1. _____

2. _____

3) Describe specific positive characteristics that make me unique and that make me stand out among others.

_____   _____   _____

_____   _____   _____

_____   _____   _____

_____   _____   _____

_____   _____   _____

_____   _____   _____

Activity: Self-Awareness Assessments

If you like assessments, there are many out there that will give you insights into your strengths, personality or your style based on answering a set of questions, for a variety of costs.

Some of my favorite ones include:
- *Strengths Finder (Rath, 2007) from the Strengths Finder 2.0 book by Tom Rath, this assessment will uncover your top 5 key strength areas.*
- *Character Assessment from the VIA Institute (VIA Institute on Character, n.d.). This assessment ranks twenty-four character traits based on your strongest ones.*
- *360 Feedback – One of the oldest methods of gathering feedback in a professional setting is through a 360 that includes feedback from your manager, peers and direct reports. You can create your own version with specific questions and ask someone to collect feedback if a formal process is not available to you.*
- *Personality Assessments:*
  - *DISC (Cipriano Training, n.d.): William Moulton Marston published his behavioral theory about DISC personality styles in 1928. In all my leadership trainings, 99.9% of people find it extremely accurate.*
  - *Myers-Briggs Type Indicator: Described by C. G. Jung, this assessment separates people into 16 distinct combinations of four preferences. (The Myers Briggs Foundation, n.d.)*
  - *Hogan Assessment: (Hogan Assessments, n.d.) In-depth personality analysis, could include blind spots based on your style and most important motives, values, and preferences. These assessments require a Hogan Certified Coach to interpret and understand.*

Not everybody is born knowing what they are good at, nor is everyone lucky enough to have people constantly point out their strengths. If you're one of the lucky few, then be extremely grateful. For many, it's a journey that leads us to finding our true strengths, gifts, or the value we bring to the world in our own unique way.

The most important reason you need to know your strengths is that almost everything in your life should revolve around them. Your success depends on you leveraging your strengths and maximizing their use.

In fact, the best choices you have available should be wrapped around your strengths:

- What are you dedicating most of your time to?
- What options for work or projects do you have based on your strengths?
- How can you share these strengths with others?
- What do these strengths look like in your personal life?
- How often are you leveraging your strengths?

Keep all of these questions in mind. If you are not spending enough time using your strengths, then consider your choices. Could spending more time on your strengths add quality to your life?

HOW ARE YOU PERCEIVED?

Perception is a reality. You may want to tell yourself that it doesn't matter what people think about you because they are "wrong." The truth is, if someone else believes something to be true about you, then this is their truth and their reality.

You can either choose to be aware of what the different versions of their truth are, or you can choose to live your life not knowing. However, for as long as these people are in your life in one way or another, "their truth" will exist. At this time, you need to choose what impact you want it to have on your life.

Tyra is now aware of the perception other people in her hospital have of her. While still very confused about **WHY they think the way**

they do, at least she knows the truth. She now has to think about what her options are and decide what she will do with this information.

WHAT ARE YOUR GAPS?

Focusing on weaknesses is pointless. Instead, it's important to define your gaps, which are limitations in the context of your goals and how you want to define yourself. There is no need to dwell on the list of things that may potentially make us "imperfect." The goal here is to focus on our goals and what we can do to *close the gap* between where we are today and where we want to be. Consider the activity below to brainstorm specific gaps that you will need to overcome.

Activity: Closing Your Gaps

Part 1 — *As you reflect on the previous chapter's ideas of what you want to define you, use a fish diagram to write down a list of what you will need to get you from here to there and close one key gap. Refer to the sample on the next page for ideas.*

Examples of gaps: *education, specific skills, critical experiences, new languages, new surroundings, new people in your network, financial stability, changing perceptions, or many other examples may apply to your situation.*

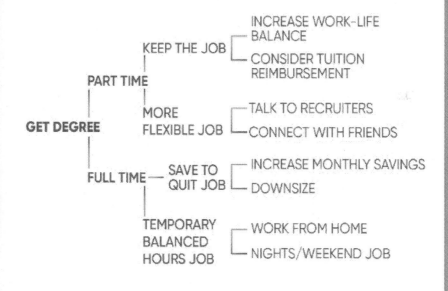

Part 2 — *Circle the most realistic ways to close this gap and draft ideas to attain them.*

1. _____

2. _____

Remember, at the end of the day it all comes down to choices. Choosing to be intentional, to be vulnerable, and to document your current limitations or obstacles is not easy. In fact, it takes great courage. Marshall Goldsmith speaks in terms of tactics when he says: *What got you here won't get you there.* He provides ideas and tips on how to think differently to move ahead (Reiter, 2007). You need to choose to face the reality of where you are before you can make concrete plans to change for the better.

These gaps, in the form of current limitations or obstacles, are all in context. I've learned from many people in my life that these need not define you either—you just have to think differently about how you can remove them or go around them.

For a lesson on physical limitations, you need to look no further than to the story of Kyle Maynard (Kyle Maynard, n.d.). Kyle was born with a rare condition that prevented the development of his fetal limbs. Despite having no limbs, his dream of being an athlete pushed him to find other less obvious ways to get around his limitations.

Kyle has achieved many things and played many sports but is most known for climbing Mount Kilimanjaro without the aid of any prosthetics. It goes without saying that his strengths of determination and resilience must've played a major role in his ability to close his physical gaps. But when you listen to him telling his story, you uncover that it all started with how he defined himself. Even though he looks physically disabled, in his mind, he is not (Heninger, 2013).

For Tyra, it was critical that she improve her ability to communicate and connect with her patients in order to influence their decisions. Communicating facts was no longer enough. She knew that this gap would be essential to figure out if she wanted to be successful in her career.

Whatever your list of current gaps includes, you still have options regarding what you do about them, how you think about them, and how you let them impact your life now or in the future.

WHY DO YOU DO WHAT YOU DO?

The next challenge is choosing to reflect on why it is that you do what you do. It's not as easy as it sounds. Sometimes this takes digging deep inside your soul to ask many *whys* in order to truly arrive at a root cause. There are many reasons that could explain your actions and behaviors. Let's explore some of the most common ones.

But before that, it's worth considering how external inputs affect how you think. Petter Johansson's TED Talk "Do you really know why you do what you do?" explores interesting concepts (Johansson, 2016). It implies that we are sometimes oblivious to how external factors influence or even change our opinions without us knowing.

Consider the implications of how some current external factors affect how you think and what you do. The great news, though, is that, as Petter says, "We are more flexible than we think. We can change our minds. Our attitudes are not set in stone."

Overused strengths: This is one of the most common explanations for unwanted behaviors. It is also one of the biggest blind spots that people have. An overused strength is a strength that you are using to the extreme, so that it's causing you harm. Like the saying goes: "Everything is better in moderation."

For Tyra, this explains a few things. First of all, she is very detail oriented, which she knows. This also explains that her personality style is to be more task-focused versus people-focused in general. It doesn't mean she doesn't care about people, but her primary focus will typically be on the details—tasks, numbers, facts, processes, instructions, design elements, etc.

So what is she doing wrong? Well, she's so focused on the details that she's overemphasizing them in her communications with her patients instead of balancing the details with the "people" needs of her patients. Similarly, people that are very people-focused sometimes miss the details because they are too focused on connecting and building relationships.

Activity: Strength Spectrum

Part 1 — Identify your top three to five strengths, based on what you know and what others might have shared with you.

_____   _____   _____

_____   _____   _____

Part 2 — Draw a line on a page for each of your strengths. Think of this line as a spectrum. On one end, consider what it looks like when you NEVER demonstrate this strength. On the other end, consider what it looks like when you ALWAYS demonstrate this strength.

ORGANIZED

NEVER   ALWAYS

⊖ DISORGANIZED   INFLEXIBLE ⊖
⊖ CONFUSED   RIGID ⊖
⊕ SPONTANEOUS   EFFICENT ⊕
⊕ FLEXIBLE   STRUCTURED ⊕

Reflect on: Put a dot on where you are on the spectrum. Put a line to reflect where you want to be. What are the consequences and implications of where you are and where you want to be? Think of the extreme sides of the spectrum as the mirror to your potential blind spots.

Upbringing assumptions and influence — In the first chapter, we explored myths that you might've been living as a result of life's experiences and the people you might've encountered along the way. These myths could be the reason why you do certain things. Have you considered that possibility?

- How similar are your beliefs to those of your parents or of the people around you?
- Have you ever questioned whether you might believe in a different or any religion at all if you had never been exposed to any growing up?
- How similar are your political beliefs to those around you?
- Do you still eat the same kind of breakfast you had growing up, or have your experiences drastically changed your preferences?
- Did the way you grew up influence how you think about education, sports, or friendships?

Experience shapes us each and every day. The people that come in and out of our lives impact how we think and act as well.

Unclear expectations — Sometimes people just default to doing what they think that others want them to do. However, many times, people are making decisions based on assumptions that may or may not be accurate.

When I ask people in my trainings how many have asked their managers what "above and beyond" means, about 3–5 percent raise their hands. The rest have made assumptions about knowing what is expected or desired. The worst part is that their goals and decisions are only based on assumptions and they may be headed down a wrong path.

Story Part 2: Controlled by a Blind Spot

Tyra spent many weeks reflecting on what had happened in the hospital. She was convinced that she had to turn around perceptions and improve her relationship with her patients.

(continued)

After realizing that she was overusing her strength—attention to detail—she decided to find a way to use that same strength to focus her attention on her patients. With such a high attention to detail, she came up with a list of things that she would learn from each new patient.

Things didn't change overnight, but she didn't give up. She took the time over the next couple of years to learn her patients' life goals, challenges, and preferred communication styles. Then she used this information to better inform how she informed and influenced her patients.

After a while, the raving feedback from her patients was all anyone at the hospital would talk about. She had uncovered a very unique way to connect with her patients using her strength. As a result of her unusual approach, she was recognized by her peers and the perception that once existed about her began to transform.

Chapter Summary

As a recap of everything we just covered, I encourage you to become keenly aware of your strengths and the value that you bring. The clearer you are, the more you can understand the choices that will bring you closest to what you want in life.

However, knowing your strengths is not enough. Being vulnerable and acknowledging the gaps to get to the goals you want is also important. Focus on the key gaps that will bring you the biggest value out of what you want.

You should get out of your comfort zone and seek to understand how others perceive you. Knowing the truth is freeing. It's not always easy to receive and it may hurt to hear. However, knowledge is power. Once you know, you can be clearer on what choices you need to make to either encourage or change those perceptions. It may sound unlikely, but sometimes seeking feedback from your toughest critics can lead you to your biggest personal transformation.

Lastly, keep digging deeper to uncover the reasons why you do what you do or think the way you do. Balance your use of strengths so that they don't become overused, and pressure-test preexisting assumptions or beliefs. All of this self-awareness will guide you as you explore the other choices you can explore to live a life without regrets.

<u>CHOICE 3 - PERSPECTIVE</u>

When you put your perspective in a blender,

you're left with many combinations of options to

pick from...

Being armed with insights about what makes you who you are and why you do what you do is very powerful. Once you have those insights, you can explore your options with better perspective—even if it takes flipping things upside down sometimes.

However, it's not always as easy as it seems. For most of us, it takes practice to consider different ways to look at things. The common expression of separating the forest from the trees implies that there are only two options – the forest and the trees. And yet, there are trees with no forest and forests with much more than trees. **It takes having a completely open mind and starting with a blank slate to consider all the possibilities.**

Story Part 1 — In the Box Thinking

Carissa was in her early forties and frustrated at work. She had been with her marketing company since it was a startup twelve years earlier and was anxiously eager to get one of the few manager roles in the company. However, no matter what she did, someone else seemed to keep getting any position that opened up.

The company had grown to thirty-five people, and every year her goal seemed to drift further away from her reach. One morning, after arriving at work, the CEO called an all-company meeting. The CEO announced that they would be moving forward with removing all job titles in an effort to increase collaboration and trust and reduce bureaucracy.

"It figures!" Carissa thought to herself. She was suddenly confronted with the fact that her dream might never come true or she would need to find another job elsewhere to become a manager.

(continued)

That afternoon, Carissa called her old mentor Jack to vent and get some advice. In the meantime, she mustered up the energy to get through the day by distracting herself with mundane work.

Carissa arrived at the corner café early the next morning and was happy to see Jack had already gotten there. "Hi, Carissa! How are you doing?" asked Jack.

"Terrible, Jack. You won't believe what's happening at the company after you left. It's so disappointing—I'm afraid I'll need to start looking for a job somewhere else."

"Wow! That bad? What happened?" asked Jack. Carissa went on to explain her history trying to get promoted, getting passed up, and now the new direction with moving toward no job titles.

(continued)

Carissa explained: "It's like you've heard before—you can be a big fish in a small pond or a small fish in a big lake. I'm not ok with being a small fish—I've been working to be a manager for so long! This isn't fair."

"But I thought you loved your job?" asked Jack. "I do! That's what's the most frustrating of all. And I love the company! I can't imagine working for another company or doing other work. I love it so much. I'm really sad that I'll have to leave it all behind," said Carissa as she exhaled with a deep sigh.

"So let me make sure I'm understanding correctly. You love what you do. You love the company. You can't imagine doing anything else or working for anyone else. And yet—you feel the need to get a new job somewhere else? I don't understand. Why do you want to be a manager so badly?" asked Jack with a confused look on his face.

(continued)

Carissa looked at him, puzzled. "Well, to get ahead, of course. If I can't grow my career here, then I can't stay." Jack sat quietly for a moment as he reflected on her comment. "So you think your only way to grow your career is to become a manager?" asked Jack.

"Well . . . Yes, I think so. I deserve it. I've worked very hard for so many years. I know I'm ready," said Carissa in an agitated tone. "Why is it so hard to understand?"

"Let's assume you get a manager job with another company. How is it going to change how you feel?" asked Jack. "Well, I'll be happier because I'll be a manager," chuckled Carissa.

"Dig a little deeper, Carissa. What is it about having that title that is going to make you happier, and why?" questioned Jack.

(continued)

"Well, I guess I think people will think highly of me and my parents would be proud of me," said Carissa. "Do you really think your parents won't be proud of you if you are not a manager? What do you think your parents would want for you?" asked Jack. Carissa started to feel uncomfortable with all the questions. She was confused about why Jack didn't understand her point of view and kept questioning her.

That night, after tucking the kids in and settling into her comfy bed, her mind wouldn't stop wondering. "What if Jack is right? Am I missing something? Should I be thinking about this differently?"

She tossed and turned for a few hours, until it finally hit her. She already had her dream job working at her dream company! Why had she not seen that before? How could she have been so blinded by her pursuit of a job title? How did she ever get there? And more than anything—what now?

In my many years in human resources, I've met many people like Carissa at all levels—from young college hires to senior leads. It's not uncommon for people to be focused on a very specific goal such as a job title, a specific role, or a specific amount of money. However, this is a very narrow focus. Let's talk through your options and how you can think through your own situation.

WHAT IS YOUR ATTITUDE?

The book that profoundly changed how I think about my attitude is *Fish!* by Stephen Lundin. At the time, I was a young professional figuring out my way around the professional world. I had never considered the fact that I had a daily choice in what my attitude would be. I had been used to letting people, events, situations, and surroundings impact how I felt and therefore how I acted.

We all have good and bad days—amazing days, terrible days, days we wish we could erase, days we wish we could crawl under the covers, and days we just go through our routine. The challenge is that everything we do, what we say, and how we act all have the potential to cause ripple effects on others around us. So, we must choose wisely what our attitude will be on a daily basis—sometimes even hourly.

This doesn't mean that we will be perfect, that we should pretend things are great when they aren't, or that we shouldn't stand up for what we believe. It means that you will start to choose to be intentional about how and when you act in certain ways that you deem fit for your circumstances. Remember, the goal is Zero Regrets. As long as you feel you acted in the best way possible at the time given the options you had, then you did the best you could, and you shouldn't have regrets. However, you can always learn from mistakes and prevent them in the future.

One of the worst things you can do is to lie to yourself by thinking that you had no other choice and take the easy way out. This is what Carissa did. She assumed the worst in a very narrow view of her reality. In fact, she was about to give up a great job at a great company without really considering the big picture and all her options.

Here are some techniques for you to consider when you are in the moment and you sense things will go awry—or they already have, and you need to reconcile your attitude for the next few minutes, hours, or days.

Activity: Practicing Positive Thinking

Daily Tips: Start your day by listening to positive affirmations, watching positive thinking videos, or reading mindfulness quotes. This will build your resilience muscle and train your brain for more positive reactions. There are many apps you can download for this, or search within Google, YouTube, Twitter, Instagram, or Facebook for people or organizations to follow.

Research the option that is most appealing to you. Write down your most common thoughts right now and what you would like to change. Commit to one of these daily tips to start your day for thirty days. Compare your notes from when you started to how you feel afterward.

Daily Tip to Follow: _____

Current Thinking I want to Change:

_____

_____

_____

Activity: Pausing in the Moment

In the Moment: *When confronted with a negative situation, P-A-U-S-E. Pausing allows for time to think before you act. For some people, it takes training to get used to it. Remember these tips:*

✓ *Patience — Have patience to know that you will uncover more options than the ones that seem immediately available.*

✓ *Assumptions — Take the time to make yourself aware of what assumptions you are making.*

✓ *Understanding — It's OK to be unsure of how to proceed right away—ask questions to increase your understanding.*

✓ *Solutions — All possibilities are not always obvious. Review different points of view before narrowing your list of solutions.*

✓ *Execute — For major decisions, "sleep on it"—wait twenty-four hours to allow for time to digest your ideas before you execute them.*

Try it once a day for the next week and see how you feel. Consider whether your decision-making changed as a result of pausing.

HOW DO YOU DEFINE SUCCESS?

Have you considered what success actually means to you? If so, why is it that you define success that way? Having goals is critical to having a forward-thinking mindset. However, focusing on the wrong goal can derail you from achieving the real goals you need in your life. As you saw with Carissa, she was about to make a big mistake. She was narrowly focused on her outcome as opposed to the experience, how she would feel, or how it would impact her life.

At work, sometimes we define success by our ability attain a specific job, a certain job title, or an ideal salary. These are not wrong but limiting—and a very common starting place for most people. When you expand your possibilities, you can include things like: 1) experiences you would like to have, 2) ways you would like to feel, 3) people you would want to work with, 4) impact you would want to make, or 5) things you want to learn. You can add many others to this list.

What is certain is that your choices have now increased to a point where you can achieve more than one, and even achieve multiple at the same time in multiple ways, without being limited by only a few options that may or may not be readily available to you.

At home, the situation is similar and yet more complex. We have multiple choices to make that impact the quality of our life, our habits, our hobbies, our interests, our health, etc.

Sometimes the problem with your current situation is that you are not seeing the possibilities. Consider all the different outcomes that you are seeking from a situation and push yourself to test out whether you are focused on the right one by comparing to others.

But how can you start to change your perspective on how you look at things? That's the hard part. Sometimes it helps to have specific things you can do when you're up against a specific point of view that needs altering. Consider the following:

- If the opposite of *yes* is not *no*, but *not yes*, then you can consider possibilities that include *maybe, possibly, partially*, and *if XYZ*, and *when XYZ* as examples.

- If the alternative to getting what you want is not *not getting it*, but *getting it partially*, then you have more possibilities to consider.

- If the opposite of *now* is not just *later*, but *not now*, that means that you can consider *increments, gradually, milestones*, and *steps* to focus your attention on.

- If instead of asking *why* or *why not*, you focus on asking *how* might you do something, you can change your perspective from limitations to actions.

- If the opposite of *knowing everything* is not *not knowing*, you can instead ask questions like "Who might know?" "How much do you need to know?" or "What questions are most important to ask?"

Activity: Negotiating for Alternatives

When you have a specific setback that you need to consider different perspectives for, try the following to negotiate your options:

✓ *Questions you can ask to consider your possibilities:*
   ○ _____
   ○ _____
   ○ _____

✓ *Partial ways you can achieve this:*
   ○ _____
   ○ _____
   ○ _____

✓ *Steps you can take to get you gradually closer to your goal:*
   ○ *Step 1* _____
   ○ *Step 2* _____
   ○ *Step 3* _____

✓ *People that can help you brainstorm other options or ideas:*
   ○ _____
   ○ _____
   ○ _____

WHEN SHOULD YOU CONSIDER REINVENTING YOURSELF?

Every so often, it's important to keep reinventing yourself. The notion of reinventing includes doing a "refresh" on one or more areas of your life. This is key to your development and growth as an individual. The world is constantly changing around us, and we know it's certain that change will continue to happen. You need to evolve with it. In addition, sometimes smaller reinventions are needed just to reenergize you.

Here are some things to consider as you decide whether the timing is right for you to reinvent yourself.

Another Hat — Are there other passions you are interested in besides the things you are currently doing? If so, it may be time for you to consider another hat. This doesn't mean you need to drop everything you are doing. Instead, it means you can find new ways to bring out your best self. For some examples, consider these questions:

- Can you take up a hobby doing something you love or excel at?
- What can you do to help people on the side, leveraging one of your strengths—either through coaching, training, or pro-bono work?
- Can you freelance doing some of this work as a side business? Or change your business and career altogether?
- Can you take training or certifications to increase skills in something new or different than what you're known for?

Another Place — Another way to look at this is by examining whether you can share some of your strengths in a different location. This means that you can still leverage what you are good at but find a new place do to it. For some examples, consider these:

- Which other organizations, companies, or general locations may value your strengths and the value you bring more than the place you are currently at?
- Which organizations or groups in addition to where you are could benefit from the value you bring to the table?
- Which different geographical locations could you explore?

Another Audience — Lastly, sometimes you don't need to change a location or your hat, but your audience. This means that you can find new people to share your message and your value with. The goal here is to reenergize through people.

- Which different groups of people would be interested in your message?
- Where could you volunteer to share the value you bring?
- Where else can you reach people that support your message and value?

What you need to keep in mind is that it's critical to evolve. We must all grow over time to stay relevant, to add value and to keep getting better at whatever we do. It's not essential to re-invent yourself and it's ok to continue doing exactly what you are doing where you are doing it. However, it's not an option to stop growing. If you stop learning, you stop evolving and you will become obsolete and will lose energy over time.

Activity: Reinventing Yourself

For this activity, start by identifying which of the three types of changes you want to make as you reinvent yourself. Then, for the ones you selected, review some of the options underneath.

New Hat:

___New Skill/Value   ___New Talent   ___New Brand
___New Perception   ___New Interest   ___New Passion

New Place:

___New Organization   ___New Job   ___New Company
___New City   ___New Country   ___New Building

New Audience:

___New Friends   ___New Coworkers   ___New Neighbors
___New Fans   ___New Clients   ___New Support

Reflection: As you review each one, consider what you need to do for that reinvention individually. Most importantly, though, consider what the combination of the changes you want can look like together.

For a new hat — How can you get started in creating that new hat? If the answer is not obvious, enlist the help of others around you. For a new place or audience, contact a few people that fall under that category to get the conversation started.

Story Part 2 — In the Box Thinking

Although perplexed, Carissa was relieved to have called Jack before making any decisions. She stayed in her job and let the news digest for a few months before she formed a plan.

She decided that because she loved her job and her company, she would need to find a new way to add value and make herself feel good even without a "manager" title. She had been pursuing that goal for so long that she had missed out on seeing the bigger picture.

She considered people she admired and the legacy she wanted to leave behind and decided to do things differently for the following year.

At work, she got more involved in work concerning consumer insights. She had previously only focused on the creative side of marketing.

(continued)

This time, she used this new energy to explore a new side of the company, leveraging her passion for people. Over time, she became the go-to person for anything related to the consumer and won industry awards for innovative insights.

At home, she got more involved in her community through volunteering, by teaching low-income children to be creative and explore careers in the marketing space.

Jack smiled when he got a letter from Carissa years later: "Jack, you are my hero. I was about to ruin my life when I talked to you that day about the changes in the company. I am so thankful for your insights and perspective. I'm now incredibly happier than I was the day I met with you, and although I still seek to grow my career and impact, I look forward to so much more than just a title."

Chapter Summary

As a recap of what we just covered, remember to keep your mind open to many different options. Sometimes it takes looking at things from a different perspective to uncover the possibilities.

The first thing to consider is your attitude when you are facing a challenging situation. Perception starts with a healthy and positive mindset. According to research, "Negative thinking slows down brain coordination, making it difficult to process thoughts and find solutions" (Teresa Aubele, 2011). As a result, your brain sees fewer possibilities. To give your brain the benefit of a wider range of options, you must practice positive thinking.

Next, look at your definition of success and consider whether you need to expand and broaden that definition. Looking at things that might incrementally help you achieve your goal or a way to achieve it in a different way could be just as meaningful.

Lastly, it's important to evolve with the constant change around us. Every so often, consider whether you should reinvent yourself through: 1) adding another hat to your current roles, 2) finding a different location to shine and add value, or 3) locating a new audience to share your message with.

All three of these tactics will broaden your perspective and increase your options. With more options come more choices. Give yourself the benefit of as many choices as possible to reduce regrets in your life.

CHOICE 4 - RELATIONSHIPS

 The health of your inner soul relies on a

garden of positive influences . . .

A really important way to live life without regrets involves picking the right people to be surrounded by. They say that you are who you hang out with—and there is some truth to that.

When you surround yourself by people who are positive, encouraging, nurturing, and caring, you are set up with a thriving environment to succeed.

When the people surrounding you are negative, critical, judgmental, or not supportive, it can limit your potential, set unneeded limitations, and result in unwanted situations.

Story Part 1 — Toxic Garden

Felipe was a go-getter from a very young age. He grew up helping his parents on the farm and had quite a green thumb as a result. He was a quick study and would pick up new things very easily, no matter what was put in front of him.

As he got older, he studied agriculture with hopes to continue the family tradition of providing nutritious products to feed the world. He saved all the money he made helping on the farm as well as running a variety of fundraisers and small projects helping farmers learn about the benefits of an organic focus.

In college, he met Moni, and they got engaged as soon as they graduated. Living together was not what Felipe had expected. As soon as they moved in together, Moni started constantly complaining about what he did, what he didn't do, and how he should do things. The constant nagging, criticizing, and undermining started to break down Felipe's self-esteem.

(continued)

With things being difficult in his home life, he dedicated more of his time to working on his parents' farm. One day, Felipe was hanging out in his garden with his grandfather. It had been a couple of years since the two of them had talked, and Felipe had invited him to come and stay at his house for a few weeks, fearing that his grandfather was getting old and might not be around too much longer.

His grandfather turned to Felipe and asked, "Felipe, are you happy with your life?" Felipe gazed at him as he pondered the question and answered, "I'm not sure, Poppa." "What do you mean you're not sure?"

Felipe explained to his grandfather that he had envisioned himself happily married, with his own business and many friends as he got older.

(continued)

He explained to his grandfather that he didn't feel like he had achieved any of his goals and they didn't seem to be on the horizon either. His grandfather started digging to find out why he hadn't achieved any of the goals he wanted.

"Felipe, life is short. You need to make the most of it and make your dreams come true. Why don't you think you can be happily married with Moni?"

Felipe looked down in disappointment. "She's not the same anymore, Poppa. She used to be sweet and caring and now all she does is complain. I know that romance fades over time and reality sets in, but it's not what I thought it would be like."

"Then why are you with her?" asked his grandfather. "Because I love her. We've been together so long, I can't even imagine starting over. It would be exhausting to start dating again."

(continued)

"Well, what about your friends? Why don't you feel like you have many friends like you would want?" asked the grandfather.

"I don't have time. Between Moni and work, I'm exhausted when I get home and have no energy left to do anything. My friends kept inviting me to go out, but since I had to cancel most times, they have all given up on me," said Felipe with tears in his eyes.

"Felipe, didn't you tell me when you were going to college that you were saving money to start your own business?"

"Yes, Poppa. I did. In fact, I still have that money," said Felipe with a proud smile on his face. "Then why haven't you started it?" asked the grandfather.

"Well, Mom and Dad don't think it's a good idea. They think that it's a waste of money and that it won't work."

I've encountered many people like Felipe in my life. No matter what country you live in, what your upbringing looked like, or where you work, we're all at risk for falling victim to an unhealthy environment. The first step is acknowledging the situation you are in, and the next is deciding what to do.

WHO IS IN YOUR CORNER?

Every happy person has at least one positive influence on their side. Most successful and happy people I've met have mentioned one key thing in common: people in their corner. Having someone in your corner means that you have someone that supports you, believes in you, and is looking out for you.

This doesn't mean that they always tell you what you want to hear or that they always agree with you. It means that they are looking out for your best interests. Their heart is in the right place, and they are there to support you, no matter what.

If you want to have a happy life, you will need to have many people in your corner. But don't mistake quantity for quality. Having a few great relationships is better than having many okay ones. Here are types of people I want you to think about:

- Do you have someone you can go vent to when something goes wrong?
- Do you have someone who will tell you the truth, no matter how much it may hurt?
- Do you have someone who believes in you and your abilities—maybe even more than you believe yourself?
- Do you have someone who will put things in perspective and help you think differently when it seems like you're stuck in a bad position?
- Do you have someone who will accept you as you are and not judge your behaviors or decisions?
- Do you have someone who tries to lift you up when you are down?
- Do you have someone who challenges you and helps you to reach a higher potential without settling?

Felipe for sure had his grandfather on his corner. He met many of the criteria on the questions listed and was a definite positive influence in his life. Who are those people in your life?

Activity: Nourishing Positive Influencers

Identify which people you currently have in your corner and pick one of these tips to nourish your relationships with these people.

- ☐ *Pick a frequency to connect with them so you don't lose touch and keep the relationship healthy. For those you don't connect with often, at least one to two times per year should be your goal.*

- ☐ *Think about what is important to these people in your corner, and make sure you're adding value to their life too. Identify one or two things that you might be able to help them with or others you can connect them with.*

Help: _____
Connections: _____
Ideas/Insights: _____

Activity: Growing Positive Influencers

Growing Your Influencers — *If you don't have someone that currently fits one of the descriptions, be intentional in how you build your relationship with the people in your corner to grow them into being these people for you.*

☐ *Ask for Referrals* — *Talk to people in your network and ask them to recommend someone that can XYZ.*

☐ *Become a Fan* — *Observe and follow people that do XYZ well and whom you want to learn from. Then reach out to them and establish a connection based on common goals, vision, or ideas.*

☐ *Look Outside the Box* — *Where might people with similar interests and goals go? Where might they meet? Where can you meet some of them? It could be the library, an organization, a club, a meetup, or even a neighbor. Consider places that may not be as obvious.*

WHO SHOULD BE AT ARM'S LENGTH?

The next set of people you might have in your life are those that you don't have much control over having in your life, but you can control how close you keep them. For instance, family members, coworkers, or clients are examples of people that you will typically not have much control over. If they are not having a positive influence on you, they are at risk for getting placed at arm's length. For those people who are exerting a negative impact in your life but won't go anywhere—you can choose to keep them at arm's length.

What does that mean? It means that you need to define for yourself the kind of relationship you want to have with them. Felipe's parents, for instance, had a big influence in his decision to open up his own business or not. This decision is a choice. Felipe can either accept to listen to their advice because he agrees with it, or he can choose to respectfully listen but disagree and do what he wants.

You won't always have a great relationship with everyone in your life. However, you can choose how you interact with them. Think about these questions:

- What things do you have in common that you can share—like personal hobbies or performance goals?
- What value do they add to your life—what can you learn from them?

- How much do you value the relationship? How will you handle disagreements if that value is high?
- How can you demonstrate respect for who they are and what they represent, regardless of whether you like them or agree with them?
- Would you consider minimizing interactions, if needed, to retain your sanity?

Whatever your answers are, try to find a way to make your circumstances with these people as neutral as possible so you minimize any negative influence they may have on your life.

Activity: Identifying Negative Influencers

Clarify your existing influencers: For the people that you interact with on a very frequent basis, consider where they fit in this chart below. Do they give you energy when you are around them? Do they bring you support?

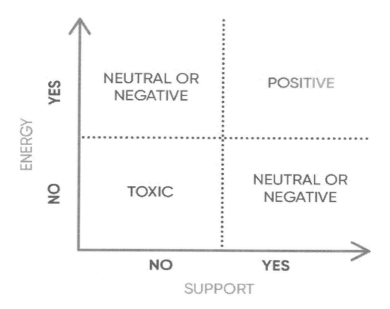

Reflection: *for those who fit the description of Negative Influencers, consider taking the following steps to minimize their impact on your life:*

- ☐ *Limit your interactions to a minimum*
- ☐ *Limit the subjects you discuss to neutral areas that might be free of conflict*
- ☐ *Respectfully agree to disagree on specific subjects and limit how much effort you spend discussing the differences in opinion*

WHO NEEDS TO GO?

Lastly, if you have negative influencers in your life whom you don't have a specific need to keep around and they're only having a toxic effect on you—they must go! While it may be hard to part ways with some of them, it's really necessary to remove them from your life in order to have a healthy environment around you. Typically, it's not entirely hard to identify who these people might be, though it is hard to admit it at times.

Let's consider this last set of questions as you reflect on who might be on this list for you.

- Is there someone who frequently undermines you and makes you feel bad about yourself?
- Is there someone who constantly criticizes you without providing any support to get better?
- Is there someone whose expectations you can never meet, as they seem to always be unhappy no matter what you do?
- Is there someone who is always negative and puts you in a bad or damp mood?

- Is there someone who is always playing the victim, blaming others, and constantly unhappy—dragging others down with him/her?

- Is there someone who stifles your creativity and inspiration by constantly critiquing?

These are the kinds of people you can do without. Learn from them, learn from yourself, and let them go. Try this exercise to identify who might need to be addressed.

Activity: Acknowledging Toxic Influencers

Part 1: Acceptance. Sometimes with these people, the hardest part is to admit to ourselves that they are only causing us harm and that we should part ways with them. Go through the questions provided and be honest with yourself about whether anyone comes to mind for one or more questions.

Part 2: Parting Ways. This is a very personal decision that only you can make. If you feel that someone meets the description of being toxic in your life, come up with a plan to part ways. It doesn't have to be overnight; it can be gradually over time. However, the sooner you remove toxic people from your life, the sooner you have more room to add positive influencers and regain lost energy.

Story Part 2 — Toxic Garden

Felipe knew he had made the right decision his first night alone after breaking up with Moni. While the decision had been really difficult because they had been through a lot together, it was time. He felt like a huge load had been lifted off his shoulders. He even felt an energy he hadn't had in many years.

Inspired by the newfound energy, Felipe took his savings and decided to start his own organic produce shop after all. While it took a lot of work to get it off the ground, it was certainly worthwhile.

One day at work, his parents stopped by to bring some fresh produce. "Felipe, I love seeing you so happy," his mother exclaimed.

"Thanks, Mom," said Felipe as he arranged the produce.

"You know, I think we were wrong, Felipe. We told you that your idea would not be successful, and you've proven us wrong. I hope you know we only want what is best for you," said his mother.

"Mom, I appreciate you caring so much. Your pushback did make me consider more details than I had originally thought about, so it actually helped me," said Felipe as he gave her a big hug.

"Son, I'm glad you went for it and made your dream come true. We're very proud of you," said his dad.

Chapter Summary

As a recap of everything we just covered, remember that there are three types of people critical to your success in having a life with Zero Regrets.

Be intentional about building and nourishing your relationship with the positive influencers in your life. These people will fill you with the energy and support needed to enjoy your life.

Be specific about how you will handle the negative influencers in your life. You should minimize the impact that these people have on you and your decisions, so they don't blur the lines between their opinions, thoughts, or ideas and what you believe.

Lastly, take meaningful steps toward eliminating toxic influencers around you. While this may be the hardest step, it is essential to giving you a healthy environment that will allow you to thrive both at home and in the workplace.

<u>CHOICE 5 - BOUNDARIES</u>

> *You are like a rubber band—if you stretch too much, you'll snap; if you never stretch at all, you're not adding any value.*

Two very common regrets people express are not living the life that they want and not standing up for themselves. Both of these have to do with the fact that people often give too much of themselves for others or others' ideals.

Story Part 1 — Extreme Help

Yu Yan started her career as a social worker after college. With a passion to help people, she couldn't wait to get started. Her first assignment was working for an organization that placed foster children in foster homes.

(continued)

She was thrilled to know that she would be able to help children find much-needed homes based on their circumstances. She would spend her time researching the best options for the foster kids and then work on getting them all set up. Part of her work was also to follow up with the kids frequently to see how they were adjusting.

After a few months, she realized the work was harder than she had thought. The children were exposed to many difficult challenges, including parents who physically hurt them or exposed them to drugs and dangerous situations.

It was not uncommon for Yu Yan to spend nights crying, thinking about those kids and how difficult their lives must be. The emotional stress took a toll on Yu Yan. She frequently got feedback to not get too attached to the kids and to never cry in front of them or their families.

(continued)

However, it wasn't easy. Yu Yan had a big heart and wanted to change the world. A few times, out of compassion, she even gave some kids her personal cell-phone number to call her if they ever needed anything. This was against the organization's policy.

One day, Yu Yan got a call from an unknown number. It was one of the foster kids she had been helping, Sammy. Sammy said "Yu, I need help. The people I'm staying with threatened to kill me. I ran away and I'm at the gas station on Main & Commerce. Can you pick me up?"

Yu Yan, without hesitating, grabbed her keys and drove to the gas station and picked up Sammy. She let him stay at her home for the night and figured she would figure out the next steps at work in the morning.

(continued)

The next morning, Yu Yan arrived at work with Sammy only to find that his foster parents had already gotten there. Yu Yan's manager immediately called her into the office to question her about what had happened.

After researching the situation, it turned out that Sammy's foster parents had restricted him from watching TV because he had said a curse word. He had refused to listen to them and ran out of the house. His foster parents had been terribly worried all night, wondering where he was. Apparently, he had already done something similar with another foster family in the past.

Yu Yan felt betrayed by Sammy and embarrassed that she had put herself out there to help and instead she had gotten played. Yu Yan had a major disciplinary reprimand at work, because she had violated the policy giving out her cell-phone number. On top of that, she was on the verge of being accused of kidnapping—taking Sammy without first getting all the facts or informing anyone.

HOW MUCH IS TOO MUCH?

Dedicating yourself to helping others is very admirable and we need more people in the world like that. However, when it comes at the detriment of you, your life, and your goals, it's no longer healthy for you. Yu Yan went above the call of duty in her attempt to help others, but she crossed the line.

Everything is great in moderation. When you are too extreme, you are at risk for facing many regrets now and later in life. Let's explore some of the more common ways people give too much.

Time — Many people dedicate almost every minute of every day to others. When you give all your time away, you leave no time to focus on you and your own personal goals. Consider these questions to see if any of these examples apply to you:

- Do you currently have time to dedicate to at least one or two hobbies outside of work that reenergize you?

- Do you currently have time to take care of yourself and your well-being—whether it's working out, eating healthy, meditation, relaxation, etc.?
- Are you spending a balanced time between technology or digital devices and the people in your life?
- Are you spending too much time on yourself and not investing enough time with other people in your life or in the community?

Financial Support — Another way people give too much is by letting others rely on them too much for financial assistance. While it's OK to help others when you are able to do so, make sure it's not having a detrimental impact on your own financial stability and your ability to save for the future. Consider these questions:

- Who is constantly asking to be bailed out and promising to pay later, and yet they don't?
- Who do you give so much financial support to that you are now feeling like you're living paycheck to paycheck, or you're now not able to save enough for your future?
- Are you enabling others to continue bad habits on management of finances, savings or spending in general?

Love — It seems strange to include love in this category. However, I've met many people who "love" someone else so unconditionally that it's unhealthy. A healthy, loving relationship should be a two-way street. When love flows only one way and negative energy flows the other way, it becomes unhealthy. Think about this:

- Do you ever feel like nothing you do is ever good enough for the person you love and you're constantly in the wrong?
- Does your stomach ache at the idea of seeing the person you love for fear that they'll say or do something to hurt you?
- If you were stranded on an island, do you think the person you love would do anything to help you survive or would they focus on their own survival?

Overindulgence: This last example is usually a result of the internal dichotomy of being afraid to not be able to indulge and as a result overdoing it. People overindulge in a variety of things—snacks, desserts, or alcohol might be the first ones that come to your mind. However, there are also other less obvious ones like overrelaxing to the point where you have just become lazy. Let's explore some questions to think about:

- When you spend your money, do you feel like you are balanced between spending on what you really need, saving for the future, and leaving a little for what you want?

- When you have a cheat meal, do you serve yourself a lot of it just in case you don't have it again soon, and you later regret having so much of it?

These are all extreme examples, but they happen all too often because we get busy with routine and used to what's around us. Sometimes it's easier to just keep things moving every day than it is to stop and question whether we're doing the right things.

Activity: Doing In Excess

For the items listed below, identify how you would rate them according to the scale provided. There is no right or wrong answer—it's all in the context of how you feel.

<u>Rate each of these 1-4:</u>
1. *Never doing this*
2. *Doing it sometimes*
3. *Doing this a lot*
4. *Doing this all the time*

- ☐ *Saving money for my future* _____
- ☐ *Spending disposable income* _____
- ☐ *Spending time on phone or social media* _____
- ☐ *Spending time with loved ones* _____
- ☐ *Focusing on wellness and well-being* _____
- ☐ *Spending time enjoying life* _____

To have Zero Regrets, draw a star by the items that are not where you would want to be to live a life without regrets. What are some things you can consider doing?

Story Part 2 — Extreme Help

A couple years after the incident with Sammy, Yu Yan was a different person. She had learned from that incident that she needed to have boundaries and had promised herself that she would never be played by another foster child again.

Whenever a foster child or parent asked for her phone number, she would only provide her work number and only answer calls during work hours.

She was so afraid to break the rules or get personal again that she decided to focus her energy on the process instead. Following the steps for each child placement and focusing on the tasks helped her remain objective.

One Friday, as she was leaving the office and closing it down, one of the parents she was working with showed up at the steps. He asked Yu Yan to help him to get more food stamps because someone had stolen most of what he had and he barely had enough to feed his kids.

(continued)

Yu Yan told the parent, "We are closed. You will need to come back on Monday and we can file the paperwork."

With tears in his eyes, the man looked at Yu Yan and said, "You must not have any kids. How can you tell me to come back on Monday? My kids won't have any food all weekend. If you can't help me, I will need to steal food from the grocery store. I can't let my children starve. It's bad enough that they have their mother in jail for physically hurting them while she was on drugs. I'm doing all I can to survive. I'm just asking for a little help."

In that moment, the man's comments crushed her heart. When did she become so heartless? He had arrived a mere fifteen minutes late to the office and she was about to make his kids starve for the weekend. She had been so focused on trying to not get personal that she'd apparently lost all empathy and personal connection to her work.

HOW LITTLE IS TOO LITTLE?

On the flip side, there are people that are so caught up in themselves or their work that they give and do very little for and with others. Here are some of the more common issues:

Connecting: I don't mean meeting people at a bar or adding people to your Facebook or Instagram accounts. This is not about quantity of people in your life, it's about quality. Many times, you go through your day talking to those you would normally interact with and potentially ignoring or passing by all others on the way. And when you talk to others, you may focus on what needs to get done or have a casual conversation about the weather. But how much time do you invest in truly connecting with others? When you connect, you find areas of common interest, you learn about what makes others tick, and you gain insights about what matters to them. If you're not reaching that level of information, then you're likely not connecting. You don't need to connect with everyone, but you should consider which relationships would benefit from connecting at a deeper level.

- When you meet with up with your friends, do you spend enough time talking to really get to know what drives them, what their challenges are, and how they think?

- How often do you make time to invest in your relationships? Do you often have an excuse for why you can't meet up or talk over the phone?

- Are you too quick to jump into logistics of what you need, what needs to get done, or how to solve a problem before building rapport and connecting with them as a person?

- Are you truly paying attention to the details being shared and seeking to understand why they are important to that person? Do you remember the details later on or write them down in order to not forget?

Standing Up: Everyone is different when it comes to standing up. For some, it's easier to stand up for others than themselves. For others, it's the other way around. Many people express regrets about one of these two. If a situation already happened and there is nothing you can do to change what you did or didn't do, you must accept it before you can move forward. However, it is still possible to consider what you might do differently in the future or if there are any follow-ups that you can do to make up for lost opportunities.

- What are some things you would do differently if you knew you wouldn't be judged, rejected, denied, or criticized and the outcome could only be positive? Is there fear holding you back from standing up?

- How passionate do you feel about your opinions, and do you make sure that everyone around you understands your passion and why?

Forgiving: Yet another area where there are many people expressing regrets in their life is in relation to holding grudges, or not forgiving someone for something they did or didn't do, and then missing out on the opportunity to maintain that relationship. To forgive or not to forgive are both very valid choices. Depending on your circumstances, it may be absolutely justified that you never forgive someone or speak to them ever again. However, if deep in your heart you know that you either regret it already or think you might regret it in the future, then the time to act is now.

I love the quote from the movie *The Green Book* (Farrelly, 2018) where the character Tony Lip says, "The world's full of lonely people afraid to make the first move." It is so true that sometimes all it takes is for you to make the first move to rebuild something that was once lost, if it's worth it for you.

- What if the person was gone tomorrow and you never got the chance to reconcile—would it matter to you?
- How would your life be different if you forgave that someone, no matter how difficult it might be?
- If it were true that everyone deserves a second chance (or third or tenth), how would it hurt you to extend a hand and reconcile to get past your differences?
- If you did something that you deeply regret, what can you do today to make things better—either for those impacted directly or for others who may be impacted in the future in a similar way?

WHAT ARE YOUR CODEPENDENCIES?

Some people are perfectly content with their situation. They don't think there is anything that is too much or too little. However, when one key person or situation is taken away, they fall apart. Why is that?

Relying on another person or thing for your own happiness can make you think everything is perfect. It's like a large band-aid over an internally unresolved problem. The sooner you increase your awareness in this area and explore your options, the sooner you can start making the right long-term choices.

Depending on Someone: When you depend on others for happiness, you are putting yourself at risk for a major disappointment. I learned this one the hard way. It was easy to rely on others around me to fill up my world with things do to, things to look forward to, and sometimes with how to feel. This works fine temporarily, while things are great.

- Is there someone whom you depend 100 percent on to provide financial support? If so, do you have a backup plan if they were no longer available?
- Is there someone you rely on heavily for their social network? If they turned against you and their network followed them, who would be left for you to socialize with?
- Is there anyone in your life who would have a significant impact on the way you live and what you do if they were not there tomorrow?
- If you had to start over on your own in a place where you didn't know anyone or anything, how easy would it be to figure out where to start and re-build?

Depending on Something: I've also met people who depended on something—primarily either a job or a certain financial lifestyle. Neither of these can be guaranteed, so relying heavily on either one of these or another thing or situation can be detrimental to you in the long run.

- If you lost your job tomorrow, however unlikely that may seem, how would you start over?

- If you became seriously ill, with heavy medical bills that impacted your financial lifestyle, would you be OK altering your lifestyle to meet your needs? What other backup would you have?

Activity: Identifying Dependencies

Consider the questions below and check off any that might apply to you.

☐ *Are you financially independent?*
☐ *Do you have your own social network?*
☐ *Do you have free rein to do as you please?*
☐ *Could you provide for your own home if you had to?*
☐ *Could you have any career you're interested in?*
☐ *Do you pick up and drop any hobbies based on your own interest and not others'?*
☐ *Do you have your own food and beverage preferences?*
☐ *Do you feel the need to seek approval from someone before making decisions?*
☐ *Do you feel the need to validate your point of view or opinion before making it public?*

If your answer was yes to all questions except the last two, then you can consider yourself very independent. If your answers varied, consider the impact of those dependencies in your life. How might you make changes to lead a higher quality of life with Zero Regrets?

Story Part 3 — Extreme Help

Yu Yan reached deep in her heart and considered what that parent was asking for. He simply needed some help to make it through the weekend, and she was the one standing in the way right now.

She apologized to the man and asked him to come into the office. She grabbed a small set of extra food stamps they had for emergencies and provided them to the man. She would help him on Monday with more-sustainable options to help his situation.

That night, Yu Yan realized she had gone from one extreme to the other and needed to rebalance. She reflected on her journey and was thankful for being able to give herself another chance.

(continued)

No one is perfect, but she was convinced she could do better. She knew it was possible for her to connect with her clients while still remaining objective in broadening her options to help them out. Nothing would stop her now from figuring out the right balance.

Chapter Summary

As a recap of everything we just covered, it's important to establish boundaries for yourself. Boundaries help us to maintain a healthy balance.

When you give too much of yourself or those things that guarantee your well-being, you are at risk for losing yourself and missing opportunities to nourish your mind, body, and soul. Consider making choices that can help you regain balance.

When you give too little or accept too little from others, you are not living life to the max. You are settling for less than you deserve and less than your potential. Consider the tradeoffs you are making and opportunities you are missing due to the choices you are making.

When you depend on something or someone else for your own happiness, it's not sustainable. You need to start making choices that allow you to depend on and believe in yourself to live life to the max.

CHOICE 6 - TIME

> **If instead of over-caffeinating, you become mindful and intentional, you might actually get something important done**

If there is one thing we could all use a little bit more of, it's time. A large majority of the articles on regrets explains that frequently regrets are related to time and how people choose to spend it.

In the book *The Pause Principle*, Kevin Cashman discusses how we live in a VUCA world. A world that is full of 1) volatility, 2) uncertainty, 3) complexity, and 4) ambiguity. To deal with all of this, he says "Our addiction to action, our busyness, our preoccupation with incessant distractions and pursuit of the ubiquitous "more" in our 24/7, constantly connected, globally caffeinated culture conspire to diminish rather than strengthen our leadership capacities." (Cashman, 2012)

With all of these distractions and mechanisms to "do more" instead of "doing smart", we can all use a little more intentional focus. Let's explore some of the more common themes and find some ways to help you optimize how you think about it.

Story Part 1 — Stretched Mom

Shima was always known for being a very charismatic, caring, and energetic person. She was very social and loved being involved in many things. Everywhere she went, she was sure to bump into someone she knew. Shima worked as a manager of a grocery store, and even at work everyone loved being around her as she was known as someone they could always count on to be there for support.

After the birth of her first child, Shima's world changed. She was a single mother and suddenly felt the need to spend every second of her life with her daughter. Like most babies, Shima's daughter required a lot of time and attention.

(continued)

Shima was overwhelmed by her new responsibilities and it soon started to take over the other areas of her life. Every day started to become exhausting and her energy started dwindling. She felt like she could no longer handle it all and needed to make some drastic changes in her life in order to survive.

Shima decided she would limit her social engagements to make more time to sleep and to be with her baby. She stopped volunteering in her community, she cancelled most of her events with her friends, and stopped working out.

A part of her felt a relief knowing she now had more time to dedicate to her baby. However, the more time passed by, the more she resented not being able to do the things she used to do.

(continued)

Her relationship with her family started to deteriorate as well. She resented her family for not offering to help more since they were local. Anytime they asked her, "What's wrong?" she would reply with an angry "Nothing," or would just complain about how she didn't have time to spend any time on herself anymore.

Was there a light at the end of the tunnel? Where could she go from here?

HOW DO YOU ORGANIZE YOUR TIME?

There are two schools of thought in terms of how you organize your time. Some people believe that you need to separate all your time so that you focus on one thing at a time. Others believe in blending the way you spend your time. Let's explore both of them so you can understand the different impacts it can have on your life.

Compartmentalized: This option suggests that you need to separate every area of your life into different compartments. It is based on the idea that your time is limited and you need to separate each component. Shima seemed to spend all her time with her baby or at work and didn't feel like she had time to spare for anything else.

Let's look at an example. If you sleep eight hours per night and work approximately fifty hours per week, that leaves sixty-two hours per week (or about 30 percent of your time) to decide on how to use. Some of this time you might spend eating, exercising, watching TV, etc.

Activity: Defining Your Compartments

Create your own chart to define what the compartments are in your life. How many hours a week do you spend on each of the key components?

WEEKLY TIME
1 WEEK = 168 HOURS

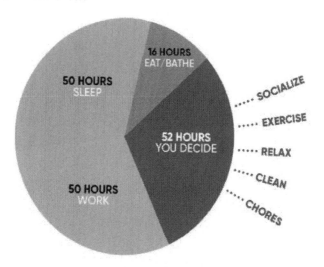

Reflection: How many of those hours do you choose yourself? Is the way you're splitting your time the way you would want to split it?

Blended: This option is based on the idea that you can blend compartments into each other to exponentially increase how you spend your time across components. It's making different kinds of lemonade when you have limited lemons.

If we go back to the example you reviewed in compartmentalizing, this is how your time under a blended lens looks like:

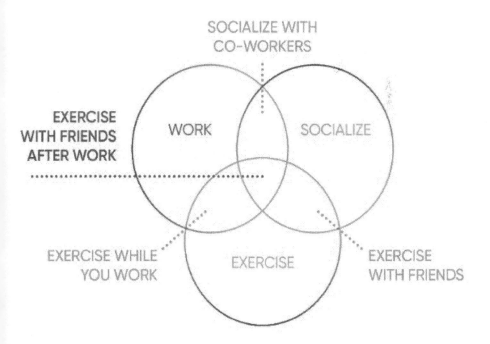

HOW INTENTIONAL ARE YOU?

As you examine the types of things you need and want to spend time on, there are two things to consider. First, can you increase the size of the pie instead of replacing one slice with another (explored under blended time perspective)? The other is to focus on quality versus quantity. If you have approximately sixty hours per week that you can decide how you spend, are you being intentional in how you spend your time?

As I mentioned earlier in the chapter, below are some of the most common regrets that people express when it comes to spending their time. Let's review some of your choices and how you can be more intentional with your time.

Family: Many times, regrets related to family regard this notion: "I should've spent more time with . . ." You may have a large family or you may have a small family; you may have a complex or blended family, or you may have a family that is very close or one that is more distant. The point is, try to define who in your family is *REALLY* important for you to have a close relationship with. And with these people, think about these questions:

- What kind of a relationship do you want to have with each of them? Do you have that relationship right now?
- Are you spending time alone with each one to build each relationship individually, or is your time always as a big family or with multiple people around?
- Do you communicate as frequently as you would like? If not, why? Is this something that you are in control of?
- Do you hold grudges against some of these people that in the long run may prevent you from having the ideal relationship? No matter what they did or didn't do, you can always take the first step.
- What is the quality of your conversations? Are they spent judging, questioning, or blaming instead of focusing on supporting, lifting, and enjoying?

Friends: Depending on your personality, you may fall anywhere on the friendship spectrum. Some people feel like they need daily, frequent, and constant interactions with people to feel energized.

Some people are perfectly content being alone and doing things on their own for extended periods of time without any interactions with others. Most fall somewhere in between. Keep in mind that you can't boil the ocean. You will likely never keep all of your friends happy, and you will likely never have the same kind of relationship with all your friends. So the question is—which relationships mean the most to you? Start there and consider these questions:

- What does success look like with each relationship you want to build?
- Are you satisfied with seeing each other every few years and having a wonderful time reminiscing about the old times?
- Are you satisfied with knowing that they are always there for you in the good and bad times, and knowing that they know you are there for them?
- Are you satisfied with the frequency with which you communicate directly with each other (text, call, email—not counting seeing a FB or Instagram post)?
- Are you satisfied with following them on social media and seeing how they're doing?

Work: A typical regret people express when it comes to work is that they spent too much time at work when they should've been doing other things. This is all in context. This is very likely going to happen to someone who is a workaholic—working over a hundred hours per week based on assumed but not justified need. If you are working multiple jobs because you need it for financial stability, it's one thing—but it's another to give your entire life away to work when it's not needed. Consider these questions:

- Is the amount of time you are working absolutely necessary? If not, is the excessive time you're investing temporary?

- Are any of the extra hours that you are working related to other people who are not doing their own jobs and you're picking up the slack? If so, what are your options for addressing the root of the issue?

- Are any of the extra hours that you are working related to the culture where you work and expectations that working more hours equals working harder? If so, what can you do to challenge the culture to think differently and focus on quality of the work versus hours worked?

- Do you have control over the amount of time you work? How many more hours are you working than are expected of you?

- If it's expected to work more hours than you'd like, what are your options? What other choices can you make or can you influence others at work to make?

Hobbies: Lastly, many people constantly complain about not having time for themselves. Let's remember that based on oversimplified assumptions, you may have anywhere from thirty to sixty hours of time that you are completely in control of. Are you saying that you can't carve out three hours per week to dedicate to yourself? All you need is to carve out thirty to sixty minutes three times a week to dedicate to yourself and invest in anything you want: exercise, painting, reading a book, going for a walk, meditating, socializing, watching a movie, getting a massage . . .

One thing is for sure—time is limited. So we've reviewed different options to look at your time under different perspectives. The other thing you need to do when making decisions is to consider your tradeoffs. What are you giving up by choosing to spend more of your time on one compartment, activity, or person?

WHO IS HELPING YOU?

Now that you've looked at different perceptions of time and how you can be more intentional, let's consider what help you need to make the changes necessary to lead a life with Zero Regrets. You can't do everything by yourself—no matter how self-sufficient you think or want to be. To lead a truly successful life in the long run, you need your support network.

What is a support system? Think of it as your very own team. In a team, people play different roles with a similar purpose. Then when something comes up, someone else picks up the slack for the greater good. In Shima's life, at first she felt like she had to do it all. Sometimes it's hard to ask for help. We can't assume people know that we need the help and when we do, we should clearly ask.

The easiest place to start could be at looking at the positive influencers we discussed in "Choice 4 - Relationships." However, not all positive influencers may be an active part of your support system, and you may have others you would consider in this space. Use this activity to help you identify your support system.

Activity: Maximizing Your Support System

Consider all the areas listed below and/or others you might want to include. Try listing as many options as you can think of to come up with options to get support in that area. If you can't think of any, call/text a friend, use Google, or post it on Facebook. You're sure to get many more ideas from others.

- *Work: How would your work be covered?*
- *Home/Loved ones: Kids? Pets? Elderly parents?*
- *Finances: Monthly expenses? One-time needs?*
- *Emotional support: Specific challenges or concerns?*
- *Creativity: Brainstorming, ideating, creating?*
- *Energy: Motivating, inspiring, uplifting?*

Reflection: How do you feel after filling out this list? Are there areas you can immediately implement some ideas in? Are there areas where you should start considering more options to enhance your support?

Story Part 2 — Stretched Mom

As time went by, Shima started a relationship with a wonderful lady she had met many years earlier. Her partner approached her one day as she sat at the kitchen table with a sad look on her face. "Shima, I miss the old you. How can I help you to get back the energy you had before?"

Shima and her partner reflected on the changes in her life and made a plan:

1. *Shima would carve out one hour for herself three days a week, when her partner would take the baby out so she could focus on herself during that time and either socialize or exercise.*

2. *Shima would return to volunteering, but only once a month so didn't get overwhelmed by all the activities.*

3. *Shima and her partner would pick one activity per week with which spend quality time together and be intentional.*

(continued)

A few months after starting these small changes, Shima started to feel like her old self. She had reconnected with many of her friends at the volunteering organization and made plans to socialize with them every other week.

Shima's relationship with her family also improved. As they clarified how they could support her with some responsibilities for her baby, they also found additional time to spend quality time together as a family.

Now, Shima has learned that while a baby is precious and delicate, it need not consume the parent's life. In fact, a baby should add more happiness. With her newfound balance, she is certain that whatever comes next in life will be much more enjoyable.

Chapter Summary

As a recap of everything we just covered, it's really important you remember the lessons in this chapter, because most regrets revolve around this topic of time.

Consider expanding your perspective of your time to find blended options for how you can spend time on more than one compartment at a time (such as spending time with family while exercising). This will allow you to spend more time in each area or reinvest your time for other things.

Next, identify how you can be intentional with your time. Life is too short and time is limited. How can you make the time you spend with people be of the highest quality? How can the time you spend on your activities be focused on the most important things versus trying to do it all?

Lastly, engage a support system to help you manage your time and to serve as a backup when you have time conflicts?

<u>CHOICE 7 - CONTROL</u>

Even a hug with the best of intentions can

be suffocating if you use too much force.

Sometimes, people are under the impression that they need to be in full control of everything to be able to make any changes. That's not entirely true. While it's important to have some level of self-control and control over some things around you, you don't need full control to live a happy, healthy life.

In fact, attempting to control too much can be detrimental, not only to your life but to those around you. Even toddlers know they don't like being controlled and told what to do. Influence is a much more powerful tool when used wisely.

Story Part 1 — Trapped by Choice

DeAndre and Irina were in a cross-cultural relationship. He came from a very dominant culture and was used to being in control in his relationships. Irina was very easygoing and came from a more passive culture; she avoided confrontation and focused more on pleasing others and overall harmony.

The couple met at a young professional networking event and found some common interests in travel and learning about the world. DeAndre didn't hesitate to ask Irina out on a date that same night, and the two quickly fell in love.

Everything was going great for the first few months. Then things started changing. One day DeAndre showed up to pick Irina up for a dinner with friends and told Irina that she couldn't wear the skirt she had on. It was too revealing and inappropriate. Irina didn't think much of it and changed clothes.

(continued)

Later that night, she was going to order a hamburger for dinner and he convinced her to get a salad instead, to keep her figure. The comments continued for months—first clothing, then food, then her use of certain words, how much personal information she shared with coworkers, how often she went out with friends . . .

One day, they were driving home, and DeAndre said he needed to stop at a friend's apartment to drop something off. He insisted that Irina stay in the car since it would be quick and she didn't know the friend anyway.

An hour later, he came back to the car. Irina waited patiently in the car because she loved him and didn't want to question his decisions. However, she was rather frustrated at the nerve he had to leave her waiting in the car that long.

(continued)

Two months later, DeAndre decided that he needed to take a trip by himself to the Bahamas. He said he needed to take a break from the stress of work and it was important for him to have this time alone. Irina tried pushing back and didn't understand why she couldn't join him, but finally gave in to the idea that he was going on his own.

After coming back, DeAndre shared his pictures with Irina. In many of them, he had girls around his arms. When she asked who they were, he shrugged and said, "Oh, just girls I met at the hotel." He said, "If I had anything to hide, I wouldn't be showing you the pictures."

Life continued, and DeAndre kept making very frequent comments about what Irina should and shouldn't do. He also asked her to stop talking to a very good male friend of hers because he didn't trust him.

(continued)

Irina started internalizing what was going on and realizing that she felt like she was trapped in her own life. She had lost control of most of her decisions and had given in to whatever DeAndre wanted simply to avoid conflict and keep their relationship going.

One night, she had an interesting thought—what would their wedding look like, if they ever got there? "Wow," she thought. "I would almost want a wedding with everyone there except DeAndre, because he would be the one person that would likely ruin the night . . ." Was it all really worth it?

WHAT IS NOT IN YOUR CONTROL?

You may be under the impression that you are not in control of most things around you. While there may be some truth to it, it's a matter of perspective. Most of the time, you do have some level of power to influence how things impact you personally or those around you.

Irina and DeAndre had different perspectives on how much control they had. DeAndre clearly felt in control and did not hesitate to control many aspects of Irina's life. Irina, on the flip side, underestimated her control and frequently ceded her control to DeAndre by allowing him to make decisions for her.

Perspective can vary for all of us. Take for instance, the weather. Some days I wish I could control when it rains or when it's sunny,—but I can't, and you, more than likely, can't either. However, I *can* control whether I get wet from the rain or burned by the sun, with a little bit of planning and intentional decision making.

The same philosophy applies to most other things in life. Let's explore some topics to help you picture your options and choices a little better.

Existing laws and rules — We were all born into the world with some things already preestablished before we got here. Yes, we need to accept that some things just are what they are today. However, if you have a strong conviction that something should be different tomorrow, you have the power to influence others around you to make changes to these laws and rules.

Laws and rules are meant to evolve with time, wisdom, insight, and human maturity. Even something that may seem black and white can have some possibilities.

- Are there specific laws or rules that impact your life and that you feel strongly should be different? What have you done about it to influence a change?
- Have you considered the value that those laws and rules bring and the reason they were established in the first place?

- Are you considering all perspectives and respecting different points of view as you approach making a change that could impact others as well?

Emergencies and accidents — None of us would usually want to be involved in any emergency or accident where someone could end up hurt. But things happen. However, the most important decisions are those that happen after. You can't change the past and never will. But you can choose to either learn from it and make changes for the better or accept it and move forward. Freezing your life in time, where it's stuck on the *what if*s or *might have been*s is not healthy.

Every situation of this type deserves some reflection and time to heal—but also the opportunity to learn and move forward.

- Have you been hanging on to any major event that didn't go as planned or had significant consequences for your life?
- If you've experienced something like this, what are some of the actions you've taken to move forward and free yourself from getting stuck in the moment?

<u>Other people's actions or reactions</u> — Many people make the mistake of thinking that they can control how other people act or react. Even parents that are "in charge" and responsible for their kids can't truly control what their kids do and whether they listen or not. They can only *influence* them to do what they want.

I've known many people who get incredibly frustrated and upset when someone doesn't do what they want. And for many of these people, it eats them up to not be able to control them, whether it's a family member or someone at work. Even a manager can't control what their employees do—only influence.

As soon as you realize the difference between controlling and influencing, you will be freed from carrying a weight that isn't yours. Consider these questions:

- Have you wasted energy trying to get someone to eat better or have a healthier lifestyle?
- Have you felt betrayed when someone said something about you that was not true?

DeAndre made a lot of decisions for Irina and she let him. However, allowing him to exercise such a strong influence on her was her decision. She always had a choice. While she might not have been able to control what he did or what he said, she could control how she reacted. She could choose to not listen, she could choose to disagree, or she could choose to negotiate. All of these were among the choices she had available.

You will have many decisions to make every day that include reacting to what others do or say. *How* you choose to react is up to you and will say a lot about you. Never forget that you can't control others— but you can always control how you choose to handle it.

Do you need to let it go?

Sometimes you just have to let it go. There will always be some things that we can't completely control. We may not like them; we may not agree with them. However, they are what they are. Exhausting our energy on being upset or disagreeing won't necessarily change anything. In fact, it can truly be counterproductive.

Controlling Situations — Letting go doesn't mean that you have to give up. It means that you are allowing yourself to be freed from negative emotions, from reactive behaviors, and from the need to control the situation. It's a choice you have to make in order to move forward.

- Do you ever dwell on situations over and over and keep thinking about how they slipped out of your hands? How is it helping you to replay them and keep thinking about them?
- How do you think others feel after listening to you mention your concerns or disappointment time and again?
- What are some better ways that you can spend your time moving forward if you no longer had to worry about how this makes you feel?

Controlling Others — When it comes to attempts at changing other people's actions or behaviors, you also need to let go. Having freedom means that we have the right to be ourselves and make our own decisions. When someone tries to control who you are or what you do, similar to how DeAndre was treating Irina, they imply that they know more than you do. Even when you mean well and even if you are right, it's important that you let others make their own choices. In the same way that you are considering your choices to lead your own life without regrets, you must allow others to make their own choices, learn from them, and lead their own lives.

- Do you ever feel so strongly about something someone else should be doing that you constantly tell them or ask them about it? Are they open to listening to your opinion at this frequency? Are their actions actually changing as a result of constant feedback?
- What ideas can you provide to influence others instead of attempting to control them?
- What frequency of recommendations is acceptable for you to feel like you've said your piece and voiced your opinion? At what point will the frequency of your opinion start to impact your relationship or have other consequences?

Controlling Yourself — The last area I want you to consider is how much you feel you need to control every aspect of who you are and what you do. It can be hard to let go of the details of everyday life when our expectations are so high. However, life is short, and most of the time we face tradeoffs in every choice we make. You should be easy on yourself. Continue with high expectations, but let go of the idea that you need to control every aspect of life. Instead, focus on the things that matter the most.

- Do you ever replay a situation over and over thinking that you could've said or done something differently in the moment?
- Do you ever focus so much on the quality of your work that you give up opportunities to work on more impactful things instead of drowning in the details?
- Do you ever choose to spend all your time cleaning because you want your surroundings impeccable and end up giving up time with family or loved ones?

In the process of letting go, you can redirect your emotions and behaviors toward the aspects that you can control.

Activity: Pay for Control

If I gave you $1000 to permanently determine where you would focus your attention, how would you split up the money between the items on this list and/or others that might be important for you? Each dollar will represent a percentage of your time in that category.

- ☐ *People — Loved ones, Friends, Networking*
- ☐ *Stability — Health, Finances, Shelter, Job(s)*
- ☐ *Personalization — What makes you YOU*
- ☐ *Quality — Organization, Cleanliness,*
- ☐ *Flavor — Diverse Experiences, Adventures, Travel*

_____ _____%
_____ _____%
_____ _____%
_____ _____%
_____ _____%
_____ _____%
_____ _____%
_____ _____%

Reflection #1: *How do they rank and stack after you split the money? Does that ranking feel right to you?*

Reflection #2: *Did you try to split all of your money among as many different components as possible or did you pick the most important and spent more money on those?*

ARE YOU MISSING OPPORTUNITIES TO SHINE?

You don't need to control everything. However, there are a few things that we sometimes forget that we can and do control. Consider these three choices and whether you may be missing anything as a result.

Stop Minimizing and Start Believing — If you don't believe in yourself, why should anyone else? It's easy to believe others when they say you have faults, you have opportunities, you have gaps, but what really matters is what *you* think. Awareness is a gift, as we covered in earlier chapters, but you also need confidence. You bring value simply because you exist, because you've had your own set of experiences, and you have your own perspective. Start believing more in yourself and your abilities without minimizing who you are or what you are capable of.

- When was the last time you questioned whether you were capable of something?

- How do you react when you make a mistake? Do you tend to blame yourself or do you blame the situation?
- When you think of your highest potential, what is it that limits you from thinking you could go one level higher than that? Is it a valid assumption or could you do more with the right support around you?

Stop Apologizing and Start Stepping Up — Women tend to do this much more than men;— but it's equally important to men. If you are spending your time apologizing for who you are, what you do and what you want, why should anyone go out of their way to support you? Instead, focus on stepping up. Show them, tell them, remind them; make it so clear that you deserve it that they won't have a choice but to agree. But that means you need to step it up. It doesn't mean you get to complain and whine until they give in; it means you influence them and convince them through determination and persistence.

- The last time you got feedback, how did you react? Did you internalize and accept your limitations, did you blame others for your faults, or did you make a plan to get better?

- Do you own it? Are you true to who you want to be and what you want to represent, and are you clear with others about what that is?

- How often do you say you're sorry? Is it only in situations where you are truly apologizing or is it by habit? Frequently saying you're sorry as a tag line undermines your value.

Stop Asking for Permission and Start Doing — Lastly, women tend to do this one more than men as well. If you are depending on others for approval, for agreement, for the next steps, you may be waiting a while. Time doesn't wait for anyone. Have you asked yourself *why* you need their advice or agreement to begin with? Some things require formalities; however, that doesn't mean that you can't take matters into your own hands and do what you think is the right thing to do—or what needs to get done. Too many opportunities go wasted when people rely on a select few to give them the green light. Time is of the essence and you should just start doing something about it.

- Is there something you feel strongly about that you haven't been able to do because you're waiting on someone to give you the green light?

- Have you felt like you may be interrupting others if you reach out, and instead withhold and wait for another moment to come by?

- Have you had the tough conversations with the people that need to hear it to move forward and remove obstacles instead of waiting for someone to change their mind?

Try this activity and start thinking about some of your daily habits. Like most things, whatever you are doing today you probably got used to over time. Maybe it's time to stop and reflect on whether you are missing any opportunities to display your best self every day.

Activity: Stop the Minimizing

Review these phrases below and consider how much you use each one of them. These are all minimizing phrases that can impact your confidence and credibility.

- *I "just" want to . . .*
- *Does that make sense?*
- *I "think" we should . . .*
- *I'm sorry for/if . . .*
- *Don't you think?*
- *You may not agree, but . . .*
- *I'm not the expert. . .*
- *I hope. . .*
- *I believe. . .*

Then consider these questions:
- *Do you joke about your work's errors or challenges?*
- *Do you start by apologizing for something that was not as important instead of addressing what is relevant in that moment?*
- *Have you considered the difference between minimizing and being humble?*

Story Part 2 — Trapped by Choice

Irina knew she had a tough choice to make. She could either stay with DeAndre and stand up to him so he would no longer control her, or she could leave him. Irina knew that it was very unlikely that DeAndre would change so the best long-term option was to leave the relationship.

Soon after, Irina met Paris. Paris was a charming and humble guy with a heart of gold. Irina felt at home with Paris and she felt comforted by him. However, she had a lot of insecurities. Deep down, she was afraid Paris would turn out like DeAndre as time went by.

Irina frequently questioned Paris's motives when he made suggestions or recommendations, and the two would end up arguing over silly things. She had her walls built up and was always on the defense.

All the arguing and questioning made Paris feel like she didn't trust him, and he didn't understand why.

(continued)

One day, Paris bumped into Irina's best friend. She asked him how everything was going, and Paris broke down in tears. He shared with her that he didn't understand why Irina was acting that way.

Irina's friend shared the story about Irina's ex-relationship with DeAndre in hopes of shedding some light about her previous experiences. It all started to make sense for Paris. How could he not have known this before?

Paris decided to have a talk with Irina that night. He shared his feelings and how he had learned about her past. He reassured Irina that he wanted her to be an equal partner with him and not someone he could control.

Irina was surprised. She had not realized how her insecurities had carried over and that they were impacting her current relationship more than she imagined.

(continued)

Irina decided to take a weight off her shoulders and trust Paris. She had no reason to doubt him and he had always been there for her. His reassurance of his commitment to their relationship and his wanting to be equals was all she needed to hear.

Now, after years of being together, the relationship is not perfect. Like all relationships, they have their ups and downs. But no matter what, they have each other's support through anything.

Irina is careful to not jump to conclusions and to start by trusting Paris. At the same time, she acknowledges that he's his own person and will not always think the same as she. And that's OK, as long as they can come to agreements together.

Chapter Summary

As a recap of everything we just covered, remember that you don't need to control everything. Trying to control everything can be detrimental to you and those around you. However, being a victim who thinks that everything is out of your control is also unhealthy and untrue.

Focus on controlling your thoughts, your attitude, and the decisions you make day in and day out. The more positive your mindset becomes, the more possibilities you will see, and the better choices you'll be able to make.

Also, don't forget that while you can't control everything, there is a lot you can do to influence changes around you. All it takes is one person taking one step forward to make a change. If you want something to be different, there is no harm in trying to change it, even if the result is only an incremental step closer to your goal.

CHOICE 8 - DREAMS

Dreaming without a plan is like making cookies and never baking them. It may be fun, but it's certainly a missed opportunity for something amazing.

What is it about dreams that intimidate people? If it's OK for you to want or pursue something, why is it often overwhelming to do something about it? We only have one life—one shot to do and try as much as we want while we're in existence.

What does a dream look like for you? Is there something you've been wanting to do for a long time? Are you living the kind of life you wish you had? Sometimes qualifications and technicalities may get in the way of you doing something as your primary job. However – would you settle for a slice of the cake at least if you can't have the full thing? Or is it all or nothing for you?

Story Part 1 — Cooking up Dreams

Hunter grew up in a home where his mom cooked marvelous meals every day. His mom loved cooking and passed on the passion to Hunter. The smell of garlic roasting, fresh basil and spices in the air, filled Hunter with dreams of one day being a chef and making mouth-watering dishes for the world.

As Hunter got older, his family ran into financial difficulties. He couldn't afford to go to culinary school, so he settled for a bachelor's degree in liberal arts. Since the economy when he graduated was in a downturn, he ended up getting a job as a waiter.

Hunter had tried to work in the kitchen at the restaurant, but the chef told him he wasn't qualified. The chef insisted that he needed formal education before he would hire him. Years passed, and Hunter spent his days dreaming of what might've been, peeking into the kitchen at the restaurant to see everyone chopping vegetables and making sauces.

(continued)

Soon, he forgot his dream and settled for cooking great meals at home for his friends and family. Many years later, the chef at the restaurant retired and a new chef was hired. Hunter built a great relationship with the chef and the staff at the restaurant and life was good.

One day, Hunter came in early to work. Upon arriving, he heard the news that the chef had been involved in a car accident. The restaurant manager was panicking because they had a special group of people coming in that day and they could not let them down.

Where would they find a backup chef with such short notice? The rest of the staff only knew their own pieces—the sauces, the vegetables, the meats—they didn't feel comfortable putting the final dishes together.

Hunter took a deep breath; he felt like a voice inside of him was saying, "You can do it".

(continued)

Full of fear of rejection, he mustered up every bit of courage he had and told the manager he could step in. He said he had worked for the restaurant for fifteen years and knew every dish. He had cooked many of them over the years at home on his own. The manager, not having a better choice, told him to go ahead and get started.

Much to everyone's amazement, the dishes turned out perfectly—exactly as if they were made by the chef himself. Everyone celebrated after their event turned into a huge success. Since the chef was still in critical condition, the manager made Hunter the temporary chef.

A few months later, the chef recovered and returned to the restaurant. He had heard the news about Hunter's cooking but he couldn't believe it was possible for him to cook so well. Hunter asked the chef if he could remain in the kitchen now that he was back, and the chef replied "Hunter, you don't have the formal education you need. You're not qualified to work in my kitchen."

What I've noticed about people who don't chase their dreams is that there are usually one of two reasons for it: 1) they are waiting for someone's approval, or 2) they are waiting for perfection.

What saddens me is to hear stories about people who saved money all their life to travel the world, to start their own business, or to make other dreams come true that never made it. I've heard countless stories of people who became too ill or physically worn to travel the world after they retired. I've heard stories of people who passed away in accidents long before they did anything to make their dreams come true.

While having a large amount of money can certainly help, it's very rarely the key to getting started. Many will say they're waiting until they save enough money, get a loan, or get investors. However, I've noticed that when someone has a passion and determination to follow their dream, nothing will get in the way. They will find a way to get started, even if it's through small steps at the beginning.

ARE YOU WAITING FOR APPROVAL?

Hunter was under the impression that a formal education in culinary school was holding him back from chasing his dream. He respected authority and as a result anchored his beliefs on what the chef told him.

If you believe in yourself, if you believe in your dream, and if you have the passion and determination, then what's stopping you? Many people are seeking validation, approval, or some form of permission. Why?

Approval from others: Validation helps us feel justified. It helps us feel like we have the support we need to do something. Permission or approval, on the other hand, implies that you're not in control. Is that what you think?

Hunter relied on the chef at the restaurant to have all the answers and expertise. When the chef said he wasn't qualified, Hunter believed him. He didn't step back to question the validity of the comment or whether there might be another way.

Pointing your finger toward someone who held you back from your dream sounds mostly like an excuse. Let's remember that we have choices regarding the relationships we build, how we treat each one, and who we keep around us.

If you think there is another person or people that are standing in the way and you need their approval, it must be because they have something you don't. However, there is seldom *one* way to get to where you are going and *one* person who can you there.

If you're at work and depend on someone for a promotion, consider your options. Do you really need that person's approval? Is there anyone else you can influence? Is there another place you can achieve what you want? What other ways can you achieve your dream where different people may support you to get there?

If you are starting a business and need an investor, consider your options. What other investors may be interested? What other ways can you get temporary or long-term funds without an investor? How have other entrepreneurs done it?

If you are seeking a specific career and haven't landed the right opportunity, consider your options. What steps can you take to become more qualified next time? Who else can you learn from to close your gaps? Who can you build a network with to understand a broader set of options?

While all of these examples include people, it doesn't mean that a specific person has to play a specific role in order for you to achieve your dreams. If they're in the way, first try to influence them. Is there anything you can do to make them change their mind? Can you talk to them? Can you try harder? Can you bring alliances along to help convince them otherwise? If all else fails and they're still in the way, then walk past them, walk around them, or walk away from them.

For those who can help—walk near them and walk with them. Bring them along, nourish win-win relationships, and don't take them for granted. But most of all, don't use others as an excuse to not get started. You have options!

Approval from yourself: Sometimes the hardest approval to gain is your own. If you've ever been criticized, rejected, or judged, it's easy to believe another person's perception of you. You start questioning yourself, your abilities, your potential, your value. You start feeling like you may not be good enough, you may not have what it takes.

But this isn't *your* truth. You know deep inside that you do have what it takes. Sometimes you're afraid to even admit it for fear of letting yourself dream, only to be let down. Well, you know what? You don't have to be perfect. You are human. And you have a value that no one else does. Your life's experiences have shaped you into having a unique perspective.

Hunter reached deep beyond his fear to accept that he may have what it takes to backfill the chef. It took great courage to believe it himself and even more to face the possibility of rejection once again. But it was his truth. He had to first allow himself the possibility to believe, to take the first step, and to ask for the opportunity.

If deep in your heart you have the burning passion to bring that value to life, then the only approval you really need is your own. And you deserve it. You have what it takes. Everyone has what it takes to chase their own dreams, but they need to believe it first.

Activity: Approval Guaranteed

You have just been promoted to the CEO of your own life. Think about what approval you might be waiting for. Pick one area where you would love to have the courage to have the conversation, take the first step, or make a move.

Imagine for a moment that I could guarantee that there was a way to get what you want without anyone else's approval. As the CEO of your own life, what actions would you take to make it happen?

Write a letter to document the steps you plan to take as CEO and how you plan to achieve what you want. Anyone reading it is not allowed to have a say or to delay or deny any of your requests. They are merely to participate in life alongside you as you make this happen.

ARE YOU WAITING FOR PERFECTION?

Many of us suffer from perfectionism blocks. If you are waiting for things to fall into the perfect puzzle, you probably have a perfectionism block. Are you waiting for the right time to pursue your dream? Are you waiting for the right feeling to know for sure it's what you want to do? Are you waiting for another day, when things are less hectic and you're not as busy?

Very rarely will a day come where everything falls into the perfect place for you to make your dreams come true. While you wait for perfection, what are you giving up? How many days or years are you willing to settle for an OK life, and only dream of what might've been? What if that day never comes? Would you regret not knowing what would've happened if you had just tried?

The fear of failure is a very disappointing phenomenon in our culture. Fear paralyzes even the smartest, brightest, and most creative if they don't allow themselves ***the right to fail***. So, let me be clear—you deserve the right to fail. You deserve the right to try it out, to experiment, to ideate—without any criticism related to its success.

If you allow yourself to give in to the idea of failure, and the idea that it doesn't need to be perfect, you can make it easier and more manageable to start. ***All you need in the beginning is a start.***

<u>**The first step:**</u> The first step is always the hardest. They say that a blank slate is the most intimidating. So, all you need to do is take a very small step. Any step in that direction is all you need. See some examples here:

- If your dream is to start your own bakery, you can start by baking some cookies over the weekend.
- If your dream is to become a doctor, you can volunteer at a hospital.
- If your dream is to write a book, you can write down some ideas.
- If your dream is to start a business, you can research your target audience.

The steps don't need to be huge. They don't need to be expensive, and they don't need to be time-consuming. One step in the right direction is all you need to take the first step toward your goal.

Activity: Defining Your First Step

Part 1: Mind map: For this activity, I recommend you draw a mind map. A mind map is a way of taking notes about the ideas in your mind and drawing them so they build from each other. Refer to the example on the next page to get an idea of how to build yours. Start with your dream in the center and map out ideas of how you can achieve it as the branches around it. No fancy software is required—just a piece of paper and a pen.

Part 2: First steps: The more ideas you build out, the more possibilities you will see. As you expand out all the options with more and more branches, try to identify what the starting points could be for a few of the different options and put a star by them.

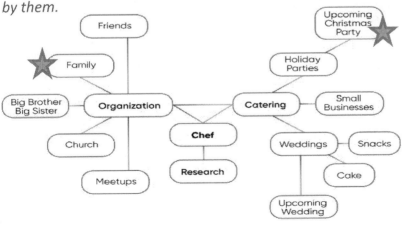

The next step: The next step you take requires more commitment. You've taken the first step in the right direction, but now you need to decide where you are headed. Your plan still doesn't need to be perfect, but it should build on what you've already done. This is where you get to do more planning and decide how dedicated you are to turning your dream into a set of goals. You will need to make some more considerations, but don't use them as an excuse to not make the next move:

- What frequency of milestones is realistic for you to keep moving?
- If you started a while ago and stopped, how can you get back on track?
- Whom from your network can you lean on for support to make the next move?

The final step: This last step is theoretical but worth considering. At what point will you feel like you were successful in following your dream? At that point will you have a new dream that takes you to another level? Will you ever feel like "good enough" will satisfy your dream?

Being clear on what the moment looks like when you will no longer have regrets should be your focus. When you know, it will guide you first and foremost toward removing that regret from your life. If the regret is only present when you didn't try, then all you need to do at the start is try. Then your next goal can be to find a successful solution. And you're further along in your life experiences than you would be if you had never tried at all.

 It does not do to dwell

on dreams and forget to live

J. K. Rowling (Rowling, 1997)

Story Part 2 — Cooking up Dreams

Hunter couldn't believe that after everything he had done the chef would still refuse to hire him in the kitchen because of his education. This made Hunter furious and yet more determined than ever.

Hunter set out to prove the chef wrong. He decided he would start by opening a small catering business. His first step was to make a menu of his best dishes. He got feedback from friends and family, and within a week, he started advertising it.

Word spread quickly since his friends and family already knew what a great cook Hunter was. Within six months, he had so many orders that he decided to quit his job and focus on the catering business.

His business was a success. With amazingly flavorful and yet healthy dishes, the demand was growing every day.

(continued)

One day, Hunter catered an event for a friend's wedding with three hundred people in attendance. As the evening was winding down, a woman approached Hunter. She was very impressed with the dishes he had catered, and she had a proposal for Hunter.

She told Hunter that she wanted to open up her own restaurant in the city's up-and-coming district. Being impressed with Hunter's food, she wondered whether Hunter might be interested in owning a portion of the restaurant and being the chef. She would fund the investment, and they would share the profits.

Hunter couldn't believe it. He had never felt "qualified" to be a chef and never thought that dream could come true. However, he had taken his first and next steps—and with every step he took, he got closer. Now, his dream was only one more step away.

(continued)

Hunter agreed to be a partner, and they started their new restaurant. Now, Hunter had other challenges to overcome, but he was determined to figure them out. He needed to hire a staff and organize their new kitchen.

Based on his experiences, Hunter decided on a different approach. He wanted to hire people with a passion for cooking and with a desire for learning and growing—even if their education was not formal. He ran the idea by his partner and she agreed.

Half of Hunter's staff didn't have the expected education, but their passion for cooking was reflected in the dishes the restaurant provided. Hunter's staff learned from him and many went on to pursue their careers in culinary arts.

They never forgot the opportunity that Hunter gave them. They kept in touch and all celebrated together every time one of them achieved something new.

Chapter Summary

As a recap of everything we just covered, remember that you have what it takes to chase your dreams and make the first step.

You don't need anyone's approval or validation but your own. Don't be too hard on yourself and remember that you don't need to be perfect, you just need to have the passion and determination to go for it!

You also need to remember that there is no perfect time or situation or plan. Get comfortable experimenting, failing, and trying again. One step is better than none. And every step you take after that gets you closer to your dream.

ZERO REGRETS CHALLENGE

The world is waiting for you to share your magic. Don't make us wait any longer.

Like the Coldplay song "Adventure of a Lifetime" (Coldplay, 2015) says, it's time to "Turn your Magic on!" If you've been completing some of the activities recommended in each of the chapters, you're already a step closer to leading a life with Zero Regrets. Now, let's be intentional with your time and make a plan to become free from regrets as soon as possible.

I've outlined a plan that will help you ease into your journey one step at a time so that it's digestible. My recommendation to those of you that are Type-A personalities and overachievers: don't rush it! It's better to make gradual changes that last rather than making fast changes that don't stick and result in you quitting before you reach all your goals.

The plan is split into the five sections below. If you look at the model below, it represents your journey. You must first work on laying the right foundation by getting your mind, body, and soul ready. Then you can focus on building your legacy and dreams.

The question is—are you ready? If not now, then when? Time is of the essence, and you shouldn't waste any more of it with regrets. Let's get started!

PLANNING FOR THE CHALLENGE

First, let's spend time defining your goals and planning your approach. Focus on attaining your goal more than focusing on the actual plan, the order of topics, or the time it will take to get there.

As you go through your journey, keep this in mind: *Progress is better than perfection*. No matter how you do on any given week or month—keep moving. Any progress will still get you closer to Zero Regrets. So, what now? As we plan for your journey, it's important to consider some things to help you achieve your goal:

Quick Wins — As you're getting started, it's important to keep it simple and easy. Quick wins will help to keep you motivated. One way to think about it is: Of all things that you have or could have regrets about, what are some quick things that you can choose to do during each part of the challenge to remove any regrets you might have associated with it?

For the first one, I wouldn't overthink it. It's important that you start with some low-hanging fruit, so you can build confidence in yourself to continue the journey as it gets harder. Let's be clear though—this is not about making impulse decisions, we want to be intentional and focused.

Here are some examples of quick wins for you to consider:

- Have you been meaning to tell someone how you feel?
- Is there a secret that has been burning you up inside that you need to tell someone about or do something about?
- Have you been wanting to sign up for something, but the fear of rejection or failure is holding you back?
- Is there a conversation you've been wanting to have but haven't found the right moment or words?
- Is there something you've been meaning to sign up for?
- Is there something you can start or stop doing right away?

Buddy — The American Society of Training and Development (ASTD) did a study on accountability and they found that you have a 65 percent chance of completing a goal if you commit to someone else (Oppong, 2017). For one key goal in each section, consider finding someone that you can lean on for support to help you achieve it and keep you accountable. It may be easier to just have one buddy for the whole challenge, but you can change the person depending on your goals and needs.

Enablers — You may need to first remove some obstacles to enable you to make some of the major personal changes you are seeking. For example, if you are seeking to break up with someone whom you are living with, there are some things you need to prepare first. You may need to figure out an alternate living arrangement. You may need to save some money to afford new furniture once you move out or to at least live on for a bit while you get your life back on track. Without these enablers, the execution of your goal may seem too daunting.

Milestones — Setting milestones that are small enough that you can't possibly fail is really important. Many times, people give up right away when they feel the goals are too hard to accomplish. Keep it simple. What are some of the small steps that you can take to help you achieve your goal? Are there daily things that you can do to start a new routine or habit? Are there small steps you can take on your journey to make your goal happen?

Success — Consider what success looks like for you in each section. What will it take before you can say that you have zero regrets for that section?

STEP # 1 — REWIRING YOUR MIND

The first step in your journey is focused on rewiring your mind. This may seem like the hardest one to attain, but it's something that you are entirely in control of, and it will impact every other decision you make along the way.

Zero Regrets Planner: Use this template provided in each step to lay out your plan. Update your Quick Wins and your Milestones. Then call your buddy and activate your first action. You can do this!

MIND

Challenge Focus: There are two areas you should focus on for this part of the challenge: 1) Rewiring what goes in your brain and 2) Rewiring what goes out of your brain.

What goes in your brain? The inputs that go into your brain are critical in influencing how you think and what you think about. If your brain has not built enough resilient muscle to take in what you hear and what you see and filter it, you are at risk for being directly impacted in the short term by stressors. As you rewire your brain, consider some of the things to which you expose your brain, your eyes, and your feelings on a daily basis. How can you make yourself physically filter out as much negative stuff in the short term to build that resilient muscle and enhance your positive and balanced thinking?

What goes out of your brain? The outputs that come out of your brain include your mindset and your attitude and ultimately influence your behaviors. While these outputs are highly influenced by the inputs, you can still make steps in directing where your thoughts go regardless of the inputs around you. For this step of the challenge, focus on the things you can do to make your mindset and attitude more open-minded, flexible, positive, and balanced. Also, consider how your mindset impacts your level of determination, your drive, and your focus. The more resilient you make your brain, the easier it will be for you to filter the inputs. Also, you can adjust the outputs to make better choices for yourself in the long run.

Activities: Start by considering the activities that we mentioned earlier in the book. You can reference the page number for the activity in the Activity List toward the end of the book. Otherwise, consider some of the new activities as well.

Existing Activities:

- Defining Your Values
- Defining Your Strengths
- Self-Awareness Assessments
- Strength Spectrum
- Practicing Positive Thinking
- Pausing in the Moment

Activity: Inspiration Journal

Start your own journal where you capture ideas that have inspired you or motivated you. You can fill it with quotes, stories, insights, lessons, pictures, poems, songs, etc. The idea is that you can come back to this journal any time you need a pick-me-up. It should be filled with things that mean something to you personally, since it's not prepopulated for the masses.

Action: Try writing in it once a week and coming back to visit for inspiration just as often. The more you add, the more value it will bring you.

Activity: Identifying Your Mind's Inputs

Over the course of a week, make a list of the types of things that are influencing your eyes and ears, which will ultimately impact what your brain thinks. Then next to each item, mark it with a (+) for those that are positive messages, and a (-) for those that are negative messages. Examples: news, shows, books, articles, music, radio, conversations around me, etc.

EYES   EARS

_____( ) _____( )
_____( ) _____( )
_____( ) _____( )
_____( ) _____( )
_____( ) _____( )
_____( ) _____( )
_____( ) _____( )
_____( ) _____( )
_____( ) _____( )
_____( ) _____( )
_____( ) _____( )
_____( ) _____( )

Reflect: How many of the inputs were positive and how many were negative? Are there areas that you would want to change to add more positive inputs into your daily routine?

Activity: Embracing Gratefulness

Watch the movie The Ultimate Gift *with James Garner, Drew Fuller, and Abigail Breslin (released in 2007). As you watch it, write a list of each "gift" that is given.*

1. _____
2. _____
3. _____
4. _____
5. _____
6. _____

7. _____
8. _____
9. _____
10. _____
11. _____
12. _____

Then reflect on your life and the gifts that life has given you:

- *What key decisions have impacted the course of your life and what did you learn from them?*
- *Who supported with something that altered how you think or how you feel?*
- *What big mistakes have you made that you learned from?*
- *If you were to pass on any learnings, lessons or "gifts" to others based on your experiences – what would they be?*

Zero Regrets Planner

Months
○ January ○ Febuary ○ March ○ April ○ May ○ June ○ July
○ August ○ September ○ October ○ November ○ December

Topic

Quick win

Buddy

Enablers

Milestones

Success

STEP # 2 — ENHANCING YOUR BODY'S WELLNESS

Zero Regrets Planner: As a reminder, use this template provided to lay out your plan. Update your Quick Wins and your Milestones. Then call your buddy and activate your first action. You can do this!

BODY

Challenge Focus: This step is focused on enhancing your body's wellness. There are two areas you should focus on for this part of the challenge: 1) reducing stress and 2) reviewing overall well-being.

How are you managing stress? Stress primarily impacts your mental health, but if left untreated, it can have physical impacts as well. I know what it feels like to feel completely overwhelmed, overworked, stretched to the max, and helpless. It's not a good feeling, and I would definitely place stress among the primary ingredients that led me to feel this way. I also know that when you learn to manage stress (as well as the culprit originators of that stress), a huge weight is lifted.

Managing your stress can single-handedly can give you huge jump-start toward a life with zero regrets when you eliminate or highly reduce these stressors. For this challenge, focus on identifying the biggest root causes of that stress in your life. Putting on band-aids to temporarily address them, to delay the pain, or to postpone the unavoidable is only going to cause more harm than good for everyone involved. You have what it takes to make the move. Find every bit of courage inside of you and take some steps to make it happen.

How healthy do you consider yourself? Everyone knows that to lead a healthy life you must sleep enough, exercise, and eat balanced meals. I'm not here to explain what steps you can make in that direction. However, it wouldn't be right if I didn't acknowledge that it is a major part of who we are and how we lead our lives. Your goal should be to feel energized, focused, and happy every day when you wake up in the morning. If you're finding yourself exhausted, in need of high caffeine levels, rushing through meals, and barely able to catch your breath, it's worth considering if there is a better way.

Life expectancy continues to rise every year, with most people living up into their eighties and many more living past one hundred. If you live until you're 105, what would you want those last twenty years to be like? Today is the best day to make some choices that have long-term impact. Just consider it for what it's worth. Again, the goal is Zero Regrets. If you're already there, that's fantastic!

Activities: Start by considering the activities that we mentioned earlier in the book. You can reference the page number for the activity in the Activity List toward the end of the book. Otherwise, consider some of the new activities as well.

<u>Existing Activities:</u>

- Doing in Excess
- Pay for Control
- Defining Your Compartments
- Maximizing Your Support System
- Negotiating for Alternatives

Activity: Get Better at Saying NO

How often do you say no? One big reason people add to their own stress is overcommitting. For the next seven days, write down every time you agreed to something that required your time that you did not absolutely have to do.

Day 1: _____
Day 2: _____
Day 3: _____
Day 4: _____
Day 5: _____
Day 6: _____
Day 7: _____

Now, for the next seven days, say no to at least one thing per day (*something that isn't absolutely critical, mandatory or necessary).

Day 1: _____
Day 2: _____
Day 3: _____
Day 4: _____
Day 5: _____
Day 6: _____
Day 7: _____

Reflect: *How did you feel saying no? Did you gain any time back from things that weren't absolutely necessary? How much more can you say "no" in the future to free critical time for yourself?*

Tips: *If saying "no" is too hard, try negotiating the terms – can you do it partially, later, or delegate it to someone else?*

Activity: Practicing Mindfulness

There is a lot of information out there regarding mindfulness. To me, mindfulness is all about being intentional and being aware. We've become experts at going through the daily motions. Some days we even wonder how we got to work, since our brain seemed to be on cruise control and we hardly remember the drive itself. To be mindful, you need to be present and be in the moment.

Over the next seven days, I recommend that you reflect every night on how your day went. How present were you in your interactions, in your actions, or in your decisions? Did you give them all the attention they deserved? How intentional were you in deciding what to eat and how much, or did you just eat everything without thinking? Did you make time to stretch, exercise, or otherwise provide your body with some care?

It's easier if you pick one topic to be mindful in. For example: Mindful eating, conversations, decisions, reflecting, etc.

Topic: _____

Day 1: _____
Day 2: _____
Day 3: _____
Day 4: _____
Day 5: _____
Day 6: _____
Day 7: _____

Zero Regrets Planner

Months
○ January ○ Febuary ○ March ○ April ○ May ○ June ○ July
○ August ○ September ○ October ○ November ○ December

Topic |

Quick win |

Buddy |

Enablers

Milestones

Success

STEP # 3 — ENERGIZING YOUR SOUL

Zero Regrets Planner: As a reminder, use this template provided to lay out your plan. Update your Quick Wins and your Milestones. Then call your buddy and activate your first action. You can do this!

SOUL

Challenge Focus: This step is focused on enhancing your soul's energy. There are two areas you should focus on for this part of the challenge: 1) energizing your connections and 2) connecting deeper.

How energized are you by your connections? This is most important for extroverts, who have a higher need to be surrounded by others. However, it's important to all. Connecting is a fundamental human characteristic. People seek to be able to connect with others in order to satisfy their need for belonging, for inclusion, and for acceptance. However, we live in a world where we're running around chasing our tails—we're so busy we don't even know the difference between a start and a finish.

We sometimes treat others as a commodity and rush through meetups and conversations to get to the next thing on the agenda. I urge you to stop and admire the beauty of what makes us human. Everyone has such different experiences, backgrounds, perspectives, and insights. For this step of the challenge, you owe it to yourself to invest more quality time into enhancing connections instead of just having conversations. What are some things you can do to surround yourself with the right people and then nourish, grow, and care for those relationships?

How much time do you invest in yourself? This one is most important for those who are introverts and have a greater need for time alone to reenergize. However, it's important for all. Time alone gives you the opportunity to take a breath, reflect, ponder, dream, and invest in your soul. When you make yourself a priority and invest that time in whatever is important to you, the energy you will get out of it will help you tenfold in other areas of your life. It's when you make yourself your last priority that the regrets start to pile up. And remember that you are in control of what you do. Don't minimize the importance of time spent on yourself. It doesn't have to be alone, but it should let you recharge.

Activities: Start by considering the activities that we mentioned earlier in the book. You can reference the page number for the activity in the Activity List toward the end of the book. Otherwise, consider some of the new activities as well.

Existing Activities:

- Nourishing Positive Influencers
- Growing Positive Influencers
- Identifying Negative Influencers
- Acknowledging Toxic Influencers
- Identifying Dependencies

Activity: Connecting Deeper

Connecting is a very personal journey. To start, it needs to be genuine and you should only start with people whom you truly care to learn more about. Next, it will require high levels of active listening. Try to make the conversation entirely about them and ask yourself these questions after the next conversations you have with these people:

- ☐ *Did I do more listening or talking in the conversation?*
- ☐ *Did I spend more time asking questions or telling them my opinion?*
- ☐ *Did I remember the details they provided the last time we met so I could incorporate it into our conversation? (Ex.: shared they were doing something, going somewhere, etc.)*
- ☐ *Did I learn something new about him/her?*
- ☐ *Do I remember the details they mentioned during this conversation?*
- ☐ *Did I add value to them during the conversation, or can I add value afterward?*

Reflection: If you tried something new or focused on something you wouldn't normally do as a result of the questions above, how did it make you feel?

Activity: Investing in Yourself

When you think about the things that really energize you, which things do you feel you are lacking in or could use more of? Do they involve other people or are they things you would do on your own? How often would you need to do this in order to feel more energized?

Investment: _____

Frequency: _____

Challenge: *Commit to doing this at the designated frequency for the next thirty to ninety days, to start. Identify any enablers that would help you accommodate for this investment in yourself. This could be another good example of leveraging a "buddy" to partner with you or hold you accountable for getting it done. You will feel really refreshed once you get started! Give it a try.*

Zero Regrets Planner

Months

○ January ○ Febuary ○ March ○ April ○ May ○ June ○ July
○ August ○ September ○ October ○ November ○ December

Topic |

Quick win |

Buddy |

Enablers

Milestones

Success

STEP # 4 — CRAFTING YOUR LEGACY

Lasting Impressions — If you followed the steps in order, congratulations on completing the foundation of your journey to Zero Regrets! How are you feeling? I can imagine you might feel a bit more energized, and yet a bit tired. The process of personal change can be both emotionally and mentally exhausting. Now that you have taken care of the foundational elements to Zero Regrets, you can focus on elevating.

Zero Regrets Planner: As a reminder, use this template provided to lay out your plan. Update your Quick Wins and your Milestones. Then call your buddy and activate your first action. You can do this!

LEGACY

Challenge Focus: This challenge is focused on crafting your legacy. There are two areas you should focus on for this part of the challenge: 1) defining your brand and 2) considering the impact.

How do you want to be remembered? A legacy, in part, includes a memory and a perception of who you are or who you were. As you work on this challenge, consider the image that you want to leave in people's minds. Also acknowledge that there is already an existing perception and legacy in their mind. Focus on becoming as clear as possible in articulating and visualizing what that memory and perception should look like when you're not there to tell your story.

What impact will you have on others around you? The other part to a legacy involves the impact you have had on others. Every day we have new opportunities to impact people around us. Whether it's impacting a janitor who cleans the bathrooms, a server at a fast-food restaurant, or a passenger on an airplane. We pass by people every day, and with every passing moment there is an opportunity to make an impact. One day, as I struggled for words to connect with an old coworker on our way to the parking lot, I dug deep to find the courage to ask about his life. He then asked how things were going for me and for a brief moment, I felt remembered, I felt cared for. Two weeks later, he passed away tragically in an accident. I will always remember him for taking the time to let me know he "saw" me. You see people every day—what kind of an impact do you want to make on them? Is there a specific cause that you are most passionate about? Is there a specific audience that moves you more than another? Focus on what means something to you. Make it personal and make it count.

Activities: Start by considering the activities that we mentioned earlier in the book. You can reference the page number for the activity in the Activity List toward the end of the book. Otherwise, consider some of the new activities as well.

Existing Activities:

- Defining Your Legacy
- Stop the Minimizing
- Reinventing Yourself

Activity: Making Your Wave

In her book Make Waves, *Patti Johnson defines the idea of creating your wave as actions that begin with "if only we could" (Johnson, 2014). The waves have three criteria:1) Impact, 2) Purpose, and 3) Knowledge and Credibility.*

- *What would you say is the impact that you want to make? How do you know when the time is right for this impact?*
- *What is the bigger purpose that engages others toward a common goal?*
- *What knowledge and credibility do you possess to start your wave and gain the right audience?*

Activity: Painting Your Picture

In order to help you visualize how people remember you today, we need to paint a visual picture. Ask your friends, family, coworkers, clients, or others around you to send you ONE picture that they think represents what you stand for. It can be anything—a cartoon, an animal, a landscape, a comic, a book, an object. In addition, ask them to explain WHY they think that picture represents you.

Make a collage of all the pictures and put them together. What do they have in common? In what ways are they unique? What does it all mean to you? How would you want to change the picture?

Activity: Creating Your Vision

Sometimes it helps to put random ideas together when you don't have the order, the patterns, or the trends figured out just yet.

Start a vision board for your Legacy. Many people use cork boards, magnet boards, or even flip charts with post-its.

Consider adding items in the following categories, and then add any others as ideas continue to pop in your mind:

- *What kinds of things are you interested in?*
- *Do you have a passion for anything in particular?*
- *If you had to help any kind of person, who would it be?*
- *What gets you excited?*
- *What value do you bring to others?*
- *What kind of help do you provide those around you?*
- *What are you known for?*
- *What skills or talents do you have?*
- *Whom do you admire?*
- *What accomplishments by others most interest you?*

As you continue going through the list, find pictures, images, words, or other notes to represent each of them on your Vision Board. The more visual you can make it, the more it will help you come up with patterns.

Then consider—what do they have in common? Which ones are similar? Is there anything connecting a few of them?

Zero Regrets Planner

Months

○ January ○ Febuary ○ March ○ April ○ May ○ June ○ July
○ August ○ September ○ October ○ November ○ December

Topic

Quick win

Buddy

Enablers

Milestones

Success

STEP # 5 — PURSUING YOUR DREAMS

This transformation is no joke. Don't be afraid to dream big. Norman Vincent Peale once said, "Shoot for the moon. Even if you miss, you'll land among the stars." It's better than not trying at all, and it will get you closer to what you want. So, what do you want the rest of your life to look like? What do you want your legacy to be? What mark will you make in the world?

Zero Regrets Planner: As a reminder, use this template provided to lay out your plan. Update your Quick Wins and your Milestones. Then call your buddy and activate your first action. You can do this!

DREAMS

Challenge Focus: This step is focused on pursuing your dream – both big and small. There are two areas you should focus on for this part of the challenge: 1) Defining what you want, and 2) Doing something about it.

<u>Do you know what you want?</u> Not everyone has big, lofty dreams such as owning your own restaurant, becoming the president, finding the cure for cancer, or solving world hunger. However, all dreams are important because they are important to *you*. Whatever your dreams may be—big or small—they are worth going for. We only have one life to live (that we know of), and should make the most of it. But it all starts with knowing what you want. How much time have you spent thinking about what you want out of life? Some dreams may be small and something you can accomplish in one afternoon. Others may take years or decades. Whatever it is, you need to start this challenge by identifying any and all of it. If you could have it ALL, what would that look like?

<u>What are you going to do about it?</u> While it's a start to know what you want, you won't get any closer to getting it until you start to take some actions in that direction. Dreams very rarely show up unannounced at your doorstep. You need to go out and make them happen. For this challenge, you need to identify as many ways as possible to get started and to keep moving. Sometimes getting started is not too hard, but once you get started, it can get difficult as you start to encounter obstacles. In her TEDx Talk, Rosabeth Moss Kanter talks about her Kanter Law: "Everything can look like a failure

in the middle . . . Middles are very difficult . . . so you should never give up" (Moss Kanter, 2013). There is a great truth to that because that's where many people seem to give up. For the challenge, it's important that you consider ways to get started, but also ways to lift yourself up when it gets challenging and not give up.

Activities: Start by considering the activities that we mentioned earlier in the book. You can reference the page number for the activity in the Activity List toward the end of the book. Otherwise, consider some of the new activities as well.

<u>Existing Activities:</u>

- Defining Your First Step
- Approval Guaranteed

Activity: Bucket List With a Twist

First, create a bucket list of all the things you can think of that you want to do or accomplish. Spend a day or two adding items to the list so you can make it as long as possible within forty-eight hours. Don't limit yourself to the space on this page.

_____ _____ _____ _____
_____ _____ _____ _____
_____ _____ _____ _____
_____ _____ _____ _____
_____ _____ _____ _____
_____ _____ _____ _____
_____ _____ _____ _____
_____ _____ _____ _____
_____ _____ _____ _____

Timing: Next, assign a period by which you want to complete each one (Six months? One year? Five years? By a particular age? Ever?).

Commitment: Lastly, make it public. Then work on it during your alone time, vacation time, birthday, anniversary, weekends when you're looking for things to do . . .

Activity: Creating a Dream Map

As a way to help you make a plan to make your dream come true, think about creating a map of options and steps to get you there. What are the steps you need to take, and when? Who are the people you need to involve, and is there something you must do before or after them? Are there other groups or organizations you must involve? Are there some tasks that you must complete on your own?

Get a corkboard and start to map it out. It may not come together all at once, but you can continue to add to it over time as more ideas come up and more steps are taken.

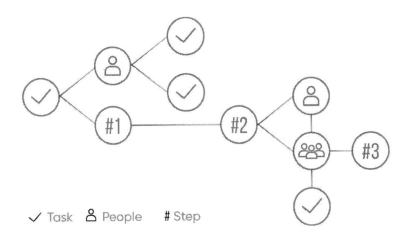

Zero Regrets Planner

Months
○ January ○ Febuary ○ March ○ April ○ May ○ June ○ July
○ August ○ September ○ October ○ November ○ December

Topic |

Quick win |

Buddy |

Enablers

Milestones

Success

PAYING IT FORWARD

We would all be in the dark if the inventors of fire and light had never shared their learnings

Like Jim Collins (Collins, 2001) might say, why settle for good when you can be great? Everyone is here on earth (or space) for a reason. You have value to bring to the world in your own unique way. Finding your value is the key, but spreading it is what unlocks its power.

Consider what value you might've gotten from the choices outlined in this book . . . or maybe the personal insights you unlocked through some of the questions. Was there a specific step in the Zero Regrets Challenge that stretched you or that you learned the most from? Who else around you might find value in what you read and learned?

I challenge you to share your learnings or insights with at least three people. You can share the book, share a key lesson, or share your personal experience—whichever one brings the greatest meaning to paying it forward for someone else.

If you're open to it, please consider sharing your stories, insights, tips, or experiences on the book's Facebook page: fb.me/ZeroRegretsChallenge. You can also use this page to learn from others or gather additional ideas to live your own life with Zero Regrets and continue paving the way for others to also enhance the quality of their lives. @ZeroRegretsChallenge #ZeroRegretsChallenge

In the end, we only regret the <u>chances</u> we didn't take, the <u>relationships</u> we were afraid to have, and the <u>decisions</u> we waited too long to make.

Lewis Carroll

ACTIVITIES LIST

REFERENCES

Brown, B. (2012). In B. Brown, *Daring Greatly* (p. 34). Penguin Random House.

Cashman, K. (2012). *The Pause Principle.*

Cipriano Training. (n.d.). Retrieved from Cipriano Training:
http://ciprianotraining.com/about-disc/

Coldplay (2015). Adventures of a Lifetime.

Collins, J. (2001). Good to Great. In J. Collins, *Good to Great.* HarperBusiness.

Farrelly, P. (Director). (2018). *The Green Book* [Motion Picture].

Heninger, M. (2013, May 2). *YouTube.* Retrieved from YouTube: Kyle Maynard:
No Arms and No Legs Climbing Mount Kilimanjaro:
https://www.youtube.com/watch?v=LuH4sK25AwE

Hogan Assessments. (n.d.). Retrieved from
https://www.hoganassessments.com/

Johansson, P. (2016, November). *Ted.* Retrieved from Do you really know why
you do what you do?:
https://www.ted.com/talks/petter_johansson_do_you_really_know_
why_you_do_what_you_do?

Johnson, P. (2014). *Make Waves.* Bibliomotion, Inc.

Kyle Maynard. (n.d.). Retrieved from Kyle Maynard: http://kyle-maynard.com/

Moss Kanter, R. (2013). *Six Keys to Leading Positive Change.* Retrieved from
YouTube: https://www.youtube.com/watch?v=owU5aTNPJbs

Oppong, T. (2017). *This is How to Increase The Odds of Reaching Your Goals by
95%.* Retrieved from Mission.org: https://medium.com/the-
mission/the-accountability-effect-a-simple-way-to-achieve-your-goals-
and-boost-your-performance-8a07c76ef53a

Rath, T. (2007). Strengths Finder 2.0. In T. Rath, *Strengths Finder 2.0.* Gallup
Press. Retrieved 3 28, 2019, from
https://digitalcommons.unomaha.edu/tedfacpub/26

Reiter, M. G. (2007). *What got you here won't get you there.*

Rowling, J. (1997). *Harry Potter and the Sorcerer's Stone.*

Teresa Aubele, P. a. (2011, August 2). *Psychology Today.* Retrieved from Happy
Brain, Happy Life: https://www.psychologytoday.com/us/blog/prime-
your-gray-cells/201108/happy-brain-happy-life

The Myers Briggs Foundation. (n.d.). Retrieved from
https://www.myersbriggs.org/my-mbti-personality-type/mbti-
basics/home.htm?bhcp=1

VIA Institute on Character. (n.d.). Retrieved from VIA Institute on Character
Survey: https://www.viacharacter.org/www/Character-Strengths-
Survey

<u>ABOUT THE AUTHOR</u>

Meli Casey is a certified life coach, human resources professional, and learning and development enthusiast. With more than fifteen years working for Fortune 500 companies, travel through more than twenty countries around the world, and a very unique personal journey, she leans on her experiences to help others develop their life skills.

Meli has a master's in entrepreneurship from Southern Methodist University and a bachelor's in business from the University of Michigan. Her learning never stops. She takes every chance she can get to learn by connecting frequently with very diverse individuals, reading, researching, and experimenting.

She lives with her children and husband in Texas and enjoys exploring unusual places and having new adventures to gather broader perspectives and unconventional ideas that will stretch her thinking.

Follow and share book stories on Facebook at
fb.me/ZeroRegretsChallenge. You can contact the author through
the Facebook messenger at m.me/ZeroRegretsChallenge to share
thoughts and insights or if you're interested in coaching and advice.

Made in the USA
Middletown, DE
05 August 2019